THE OLDER WORKER ADVANTAGE

THE OLDER WORKER ADVANTAGE

Making the Most of Our Aging Workforce

GORDON F. SHEA and
ADOLF HAASEN

Westport, Connecticut
London

Library of Congress Cataloging-in-Publication Data

Shea, Gordon F., 1925–
    The older worker advantage : making the most of our aging workforce /
    Gordon F. Shea and Adolf Haasen.
        p.   cm.
    Includes bibliographical references and index.
    ISBN 0–275–98701–9 (alk. paper)
    1. Older people—Employment.   I. Haasen, Adolf.   II. Title.
    HD6279.S54   2006
    331.3'98—dc22   2005019186

British Library Cataloguing in Publication Data is available.

Library of Congress Catalog Card Number: 2005019186
ISBN:0–275–98701–9

First published in 2006

Praeger Publishers, 88 Post Road West, Westport, CT 06881
An imprint of Greenwood Publishing Group, Inc.
www.praeger.com

Printed in the United States of America

The paper used in this book complies with the
Permanent Paper Standard issued by the National
Information Standards Organization (Z39.48–1984).

10 9 8 7 6 5 4 3 2 1

CONTENTS

INTRODUCTION: THE GRAYING
OF AMERICA

> Grow old along with me!
> The best is yet to be,
> The last of life, for which the first was made.
> Our times are in his hand
> Who saith, "A whole I planned;
> Youth shows but half. Trust God; see all, nor be
> afraid!"
>
> So, take and use thy work;
> Amend what flaws may lurk,
> What strain o' the stuff, what warpings past the aim!
> My times be in thy hand!
> Perfect the cup as planned!
> Let age approve of youth, and death complete the
> same!
>
> *Robert Browning (1812–1884)*
> *Excerpted from "Rabbi Ben Ezra"*

At the end of this decade, the United States will reach a point where almost half of its working population will be in their 50s and 60s, an age that at the beginning of the twentieth century was far beyond the average life expectancy. The generational phenomenon of the baby boomers—77 million people out of a projected labor force of 162 million in 2012—is causing this bulge of older people who are now starting to come of the age to retire. Will they really "retire" (which means to leave the field)? It's hard to imagine. The baby boomers have always been active and fitness-prone; well educated and knowledgeable; and aware of their power in society. It's almost inconceivable to see them exchange their active lives for a leisure-oriented retirement.

To the contrary—in the future, it seems more likely to see people work late in life; stay involved and engaged; and fruitfully employ their brainpower; becoming increasingly important to workplaces and society. Older workers' initiative and creativity will be leaven to society, their intellectual abilities a "natural resource" to tomorrow's work environment. The Information Age workplace and the Knowledge Society will depend on the older worker to achieve further progress. Already there is talk about shortages of expert labor in certain areas. Rather than trying to outsource these jobs or to ease immigration barriers for certain professions, we should focus on the resource of older workers and provide them with the opportunity to stay active.

All this makes it necessary, however, that we change our mind-set regarding older people and start seeing them as a resource to be cultivated. We have to shed many common misconceptions and stereotypes built up over previous centuries, decades, and years. We have to realize that the nature of older people has changed—today's older worker is different. Whether the older employee is a janitor or a corporate chief executive officer (CEO); a surgeon performing an operation or a policewoman walking a beat; a volunteer mentor helping a child or a research scientist working on a cure for cancer; a physical education teacher at the local high school or even a soldier protecting our nation—the list may go on endlessly—all of them create value and produce service to our commonweal.

There is another side to old age, to which Robert Browning alludes with the words, "The last of life, for which the first was made"—the notion of elderliness, which in Browning's times was a period of reflection, retrospection, and retreat when ailments abounded and health deteriorated. That's much changed today. As a result of the medical revolution in recent years, the older generation is increasingly healthier and more wellness-oriented and energetic. Today's older people are more able and demanding of outlets for their capabilities and talents. Their level of education is a powerful incentive to continue on that path and pursue new skills. Lifelong learning and maintaining their intellectual flexibility make this old-age generation adaptable to, and involved in, the many facets of knowledge work.

It seems to us—and that has been the major reason for writing this book—that employers in the private sector; in government; in the institutional sector; their executives and managers; their supervisors; and their people in general need to hear, become knowledgeable about, and reflect on this new situation. Older employees, because of their intellectual abilities, their social skills, and their strong ethics and values are, and will be, a special asset and advantage to every organization. It's a resource that will no doubt be available and that we should begin to understand, value, and appreciate.

To make it easy to read and capture the important details, we have divided this book in three parts—Part I is a general and introductory orientation on different aspects of the older worker in society and the workplace, Part II describes the changed role of the older worker, and Part III covers today's new multigenerational environment. Each part has its own introduction to shepherd the reader through the varied subject matters. It is our great hope that this book will be a useful guide to this fastest-growing resource of today's labor market—older workers and retirees.

PART I

PERSPECTIVES ON OLDER WORKERS

This first stop in our journey to understand, appreciate, and more actively involve this country's aging labor force must be to consciously acknowledge the wrongfulness of our past omissions, to correct our mind-set, and to start substituting reality for false assumptions about older workers. We do this by reminding ourselves how the nature of work, the workplace, and organizational cultures have changed; by examining demographics and labor force projections; and by developing a sense of what it means for older people and senior citizens in this country to retire or to continue working.

Many of the changes and developments of recent years have been significant and even revolutionary. How we go about them and how we manage our relationship to the older generation will in large measure determine the economic, social, and political future of our society.

This first part of the book covers several aspects of the older workers' panorama:

- First, we look at *changing perspectives* as to workers, workplaces, and cultures and give an all-out summary of past and present relationships with older workers. America has evolved from the ever-young nation into a country of older, more mature people, evidencing more wisdom and experience but often bearing the burden of past disdain and discrimination. There is much food for thought on how to manage this transformation and give new meaning to our relationships.

- Next, the *demographic imperatives* provide startling findings about the aging of the U.S. labor force. By 2012, almost half of the projected

162 million workers will be between 48 and 66 years old. We analyze the short-term and long-term implications and draw some conclusions on employment and retirement trends of the "older workers" generation. Certain international comparisons, while driven by slightly different circumstances, help us to put the U.S. situation in perspective.

- The following chapter on the *evolving meaning of retirement* gives us a different view, from the inside out, on what it means to retire. Seniors have many opportunities to stay active and to continue contributing to society. They should take advantage of the many choices available today and in the future for the elderly.

- Finally, we focus on, and make some recommendation for, *shedding common assumptions* regarding older people. Enough insulting myths and damaging stereotypes have been around for decades. They are no longer socially acceptable and a violation of the law. It is high time to get to the bottom of this problem and try to deal, once and for all, with the issues of age discrimination.

This segment of the book sets the stage for a more compassionate, inclusive, and participative environment toward senior workers in the future. Given the demographics and the baby boomer generation coming to retirement age, we have no choice. America is aging, and the implications for business and society must be heeded.

CHAPTER 1

Changing Perspectives on Older Workers, Workplaces, and Organizational Cultures

America has always been a young country—young in people, young in hope, young in ideals, young in culture, young in attitudes, and young in outlook—until recently. The unspoiled nature of the land when the Europeans arrived, the experimentation with a fresh form of government, the vast opportunities for the dominant culture, rejection of Old World values, and the hard physical work required to clear the forests, work the farms, and run the factories led to a logical focus on youth, strength, and vigor, rather than on contemplation, experience, and wisdom. At the same time, slave ship captains and plantation owners paid premium prices for the young and able slaves, and the Native American tribes relied on their young warriors to stem the encroachment of the European-based civilization. For the most part, youth carried the burden and reaped many of the rewards. After all, one might never live to get old—and most did not.

This focus on the young, our hope, and our future grew naturally in the minds of the people. Until recently, old age, often starting in a person's 40s, was a time of decline, of ailments and lessened abilities. With child factory labor common until the twentieth century and children seen as assets by farm families, who produced them in large numbers, the gains from youth were apparent to all. Because young adults, until recent decades, often had their intellectual growth stunted and suffered the accumulated ravages of common diseases, marginal nutrition, polluted work environments, and common plagues, growing old was seldom seen as a benefit.

Yet just as things were beginning to change—that is, as many common diseases were being conquered, the life span was extending, the standard of living of the average person was improving, retirement for some seemed a possibility, and the health and wellness of older people were improving—Hollywood, radio, and eventually television discovered the youth market, and our economic focus came to generate a youth-oriented culture. In the 1950s and 1960s, it became fashionable to "not trust anyone over 30," but youth's time was running short.

In the last two decades, it has become apparent to even the less alert observer that our society is undergoing substantial changes related to our age concepts and age realities. Gray-power politics, a significant and growing proportion of our population retired from productive contribution to the commonweal, and the aging of the workforce itself portend great changes in the way society deals with older people now that the post–World War II baby boom is close to retirement age.

Because our society and our workforce are aging rapidly, new ways must be found to ensure a longer working life for those who wish or need it, aside from the demographic imperatives, which may dictate increased levels of work participation for older people anyway. In addition, it is necessary to enhance the contribution to society of the skills and knowledge possessed by older people and to ensure better overall management of this special component of our human and intellectual resources.

We are not alone in all of this. All of the advanced societies, from Western Europe to Japan, are experiencing the same type of age shifts in their populations and are encountering many of the same problems associated with these changes, although the situation in the United States is compounded by the baby boomer generation. This gives us an opportunity to learn from each other as we move into this age of the aged.

THE PROBLEM

For more than a few decades, we have been concerned about the strong, persistent tendency for many companies, institutions, and government agencies to virtually force older employees out of the workforce or to bribe them into taking early retirement. We don't seem to understand the reality of what it means to the older person, whose talents may be badly needed in the workplace. But in a single day, a productive, earning, contributing human being might become a fallow, consuming, disconnected retiree; a state in which some stay for the rest of their lives.

Social Security funds and pension benefits are not wealth except in the minds of the beneficiary. These funds are a call upon wealth. Real wealth is the goods that we produce and the services that we render. When a person leaves the workforce, he or she may become a total consumer rather than a producer. More dollars from pension funds released into the marketplace to chase fewer goods and services is the classic prescription for inflation and economic trouble. Older people who continue to contribute to the commonweal are a valuable national asset and should be treated as such by people and policymakers at all levels.

While it is true that many people have joyfully sought the freedom of retirement as a way to escape the confinement, boredom, and sometimes onerous work of their jobs, others wished to continue gainful employment and enjoy the satisfaction of comradeship, a satisfying routine, interaction with customers, or the pleasures of interesting and challenging work. Sadly, for such people, being pushed out has often been accompanied by the implication that they were somehow not as good as, or as valuable as, their younger peers.

We have found through considerable research a set of very complex, interlocking problems related to how we manage or mismanage our human resources and the lives of many of our long-term employees, on the job and afterward. There is a great need for an examination of how those older people who would like to continue working can manage and be managed so that their productive potential continues to contribute to our gross national product (GNP) and our nation's social and economic well-being. Similar problems are faced by older people in other societies as well. In an increasingly global economy the issues are becoming interconnected and worldwide.

The elder problems are not an abstraction to be solved by some government agency or personnel policy alone. It is an issue that each of us must address when dealing with an older worker and eventually (if not now) with ourselves, whether we be supervisor, coworker, personnel specialist, or executive; whether we set policy or implement it; and whether we serve as counselor, friend, or a helping agent to older employees when they face the decision of whether or not to continue working. Also each of us must decide on how we personally handle this challenge.

The plight of some older workers faced with stereotyping, discrimination on the job, and, in some cases, declining capabilities that nevertheless could be productively employed is a very human problem. Much personal suffering occurs because of a lack of caring in the workplace, failure to see win-win options about job and work choices for older people, and sometimes insensitive, poorly conceived, and even discriminatory policies and their implementation.

Older workers are a national resource. They are most often skilled and experienced. When they leave the workforce at an early stage, both the individuals and society lose. As policymakers review the implications of an aging population, it becomes clear that they must pay particular attention to the problems of older workers. Public policy should strive to accommodate both those who are ready to really retire (i.e., leave the field of productive engagement) and those who would like to continue to work in some capacity. Institutional barriers must be lowered and innovative approaches developed. The efforts of private sector employers are the major key to success.

THE CHALLENGE TO MANAGEMENT

Until quite recently, much of this formerly minority resource of older employees—whether workers, professionals, or managers—has been, on the whole, poorly managed. For a long time, aging employees in our organizations have been largely cut off from job-related education, development, and promotional opportunities because "they're too close to retirement." With the continued aging of our workforce and the increasing clout of older employees, we can no longer afford to take a casual view of one of our few resources that are growing in quantity and quality as years go by. Perhaps nowhere are new attitudes, new practices, and new visions more needed than in the management of older employees and the opportunities they provide.

There is a second and more important consideration. In the transition to the emerging Information Age, both the nature of work and the workplace have changed, giving today's worker a different role. In the leading organizations, work has often become more complex, requiring a more democratic, inclusive, and mature approach throughout the organization. There must be a willingness to share information, expertise, and experience, to work as a team of equals but contributing different skills. Rank and privilege are no longer acceptable. Based on a sense of family in the workplace, mutual trust and a dedication to each other seem strong, with joint achievement leading to joy and fulfillment. The evolving models of organizational culture are those of truly participative leadership and of self-management where managers become role models for the organization, renounce the authority of their "office," and turn into mentors and a source of experience and expertise.

How productive our workforce remains (or becomes), the quality of working life experienced by all employees, and, in large measure, the future of our economy and society are highly dependent on how well older people, individually and collectively, are treated and, most importantly, contribute their work. It is clear that we are increasingly dependent on older workers to produce for, and help manage, our society. Above all, we need a more balanced look at our workforce if we are to gain maximum advantage from each of our age segments in the decades ahead.

To appropriately appraise this shift from a focus on youth to one on older workers, we need to deal with two preliminary questions: (1) What is different about dealing successfully with older workers? and (2) Why is how we manage older workers important?

WHAT IS DIFFERENT ABOUT DEALING SUCCESSFULLY WITH OLDER WORKERS?

Most older workers want most of the same things out of work that others want: income, dignity, a sense of belonging, security, a chance to contribute, recognition, interesting work, opportunities to show what they can do, companionship, respect, career growth, influence over what happens to them, and so on. These common desires of older people are shared with most employed people of all ages, but (as with others) each person's list and priorities are special and individual. On the other hand, some things about older workers are different. For instance:

- "Older employees," by various definitions, are a legally protected class of workers, and how management and others relate to them definitely affects the organization and those employed by it.

- Older workers often have some options and protections that younger people may lack, such as vested pension plans and seniority rights.

- The term "older workers" embraces a very broad range of people and their activities and includes many volunteers as well as employed people.

- Older people, workers and nonworkers, are part of a growing political constituency that has, and will continue to have, a powerful effect on labor laws and public policy.

- Older workers are, and for some time to come will be, one of the fastest-growing components of the workforce; consequently, organizations are increasingly dependent on them.

- Older workers represent a health and wellness influence on organizational operations that will grow as their average age and health and their numbers increase in the workplace.

- Many older workers are still subjected to much prejudice and stereotyping that hamper their ability to contribute to their employers' or society's well-being.

- Older workers represent a powerful potential for (often unexpected) productivity gains.

WHY IS HOW WE MANAGE OLDER WORKERS IMPORTANT?

Many of the characteristics of older people are particularly suited to the emerging Information Age: as their physical prowess, so appropriate to the Industrial Age, may decline, their institutional memory, ability to synthesize, and judgment tend to increase in value. As a society, we increasingly have to invest in the productive potential of older people or see unnecessary declines in our gross national product while laying out increasing sums for the forced idleness of some of our best workers. Many employers must change many of their ways of doing business if they are to encourage older people who need or want to work to remain employed. Many questionable past and current management practices have greatly wasted the knowledge and ability of older people. Such practices need to be identified and remedied.

Managing a progressively aging workforce may be one of the greatest challenges faced by management in the next several decades. The productivity and wealth of any society depend on the effective management of its resources. We have reached the point in human development where our future hinges on how well we manage our most valuable form of human capital—ourselves. In time, all who survive will be part of our older population. How well we live and relate to each other depends in large measure on how well we manage our relationship to each other.

First we need to discuss a number of key issues.

HOW OLD IS OLD?

People in the United States not only are living longer but are living younger. A person of 50 today is usually in better shape than the average 40-year-old was two decades ago. You have probably seen Grant Wood's painting *American Gothic*, in which a stern-faced farmer holds a pitchfork while his dowdy sister stands next to him. Jane Fonda, at the height of her success in selling her exercise videotapes, was, at age 47, 17 years older than that farmer's sister.

The notion that reaching a certain age renders one less useful than when one was younger is a relatively new one. Until the end of the nineteenth century, people were not regarded as old until they could no longer take care of themselves. For many reasons (some of them positive) this country has attempted to rigidly fix the point at which an individual presumably becomes less able and therefore ready for retirement. It is increasingly questionable whether society can any longer afford to hold such a stance on working age.

When the Social Security Act was passed in 1935, a presidential pen stroke established age 65 as the accepted crossover point from working to nonworking (with a few exceptions, primarily related to disability, setting the age at 62). Now federal law has abolished altogether any mandatory retirement age except for some special categories of employees. Along similar lines, the Social Security system has started to introduce changes to its general age categories. Ironically, just as Americans are tending to become physically and mentally more able at later ages, the early-retirement phenomenon in America promotes the notion that the age at which a person is classed as old is coming down.

When is an employee considered old? The Age Discrimination in Employment Act (ADEA) included everyone age 40 and above. Nevertheless, though there is no firm agreement on any given number, there seems to be a consensus forming around the age of 50 as a way to distinguish between "middle-aged" and "older" employees.

However, few people in their 40s see themselves as old, nor do most other people consider them to be old. Fifty seems useful, because many employees emotionally view the half-century mark as a watershed of their lives, and it is here that organizations begin to question the value of further investment in an older employee—especially organizations offering early-retirement options. Most importantly, at about 50 certain types of age discrimination have traditionally become operable.

Many experts also view age 50 as a turning point in an individual's career. Traditionally, an employee is supposed to follow a steady climb up the ladder in experience, pay, or position, beginning in the early 20s and peaking in the late 40s. At that point, one reaches a plateau, and if management policies take their usual course, a person thereafter is either static or moving downward, that is, receiving fewer promotions, fewer educational opportunities, and, perhaps, a decrease in responsibilities. This circumstance is based on the assumption that the individual is quickly approaching retirement or is in a state of declining abilities.

Consequently, some employers set 55 as the age when employees may take early retirement, and this figure is built into some pension plans. Thus, for our purposes, we consider age 50 as the turning point (except when legal factors are involved), though the limitations of any such definition are quite apparent.

NEED FOR A NEW VISION

To successfully adapt to our rapidly changing world, we need a new vision that takes into account at least the following factors related to older workers.

The Knowledge Worker

The age of the highly trained and educated knowledge worker is surely here and will bear the brunt of our productivity challenge for decades to come. The generation of new wealth hinges on the knowledge and skills of the Information Age worker, whether it is the engineer designing a new product by computer or the researcher developing a new material. Will our rapidly aging workforce be prepared (educated and developed) to carry that burden?

In the next chapter we see some of the occupations and jobs that already today are covered by an extraordinarily high participation of older workers, for example, social workers with about 30%, systems analysts with over 27%, and pilots and flight engineers with close to 27%. This only highlights the need of a special focus on the older employees among us.

The Learning Curve and Productivity

Every job has a learning curve. Generally, it is steep when a person is new to the job. That is, the employee's absorption of new information is very rapid at first. The person learns many things and learns them quickly. Eventually, however, the curve tends to level off as one's work is mastered or to climb slowly as the job changes or evolves. For too long, the experience on which many older employees have staked their claim to fame has often been an illusion. Thirty years of experience on a given job often meant one year of experience stretched out over 30 years, with only imperceptible real growth in learning occurring as the person aged. In the skilled trades and the professions, on-the-job learning did accrue over the years, but until the last quarter century the great bulk of America's workers have been unskilled or semiskilled workers, with little change in their job over decades. That picture, however, is changing. Old jobs are dying more rapidly than ever. New ones are being created quickly. Rapid adaptation is becoming essential for all age groups. But what of older employees? Contrary to popular stereotypes, older workers can adapt successfully to new occupations and trades, master new skills, and learn as successfully as anyone—if proper training methods are used.

Lifetime Learning

A culture of continuous education must permeate the workplace and be operative for as long as an employee remains with an organization. Cutting older people out of available developmental and educational opportunities is indefensible.

Self-Investment

Older workers must also take greater responsibility for enhancing their own breadth and depth of knowledge and skills. Each worker (and the worker's organization) must cooperate in periodically rejuvenating the employee's learning through cross-training, promotion, or even lateral transfers, to mention only a few of the devices that can accomplish that.

Changing Organizational Structures

The tall, hierarchical organizational structure has given way through downsizing and delayering to flatter, more versatile structures, where eternal career climbing may no longer pay off as the all-consuming passion of many younger people. Older employees tend to be more content with, and in some ways more amenable to, accepting the challenges of lateral transfers rather than just climbing. Hence, they may increasingly flourish in an environment that is less structured.

Information Management

Already back in 1988, Peter Drucker pointed out that older managers who have always found information scarce, expensive to develop, and slow in coming may now be swamped with it.[1] Consequently, older personnel may well need to be prepared to manage information more effectively if they are to stay on top of their jobs.

The Need for Wisdom

Information requires more than just management; it must be put to some useful purpose. Some older workers may be uniquely qualified to make sense of our information glut. If they can stand back and put it in perspective, they can effectively direct its use. Meaningful experience, the ability to synthesize, and wisdom itself are somewhat related to age. But there is a whole emerging realm in adult education where these special abilities often found in older people can be heightened, focused, and directed toward constructive organizational ends.

Principles of New Cultures

In a recent publication, *New Corporate Cultures That Motivate*, we outlined the most important principles that distinguish new cultures.[2] They are as follows:

- People's *ownership and entrepreneurial spirit* drives them to create their own challenge, take responsibilities, and become leaders, contributing to an expanding and successful business.
- Easy-to-understand *values* are guideposts, in part based on simple human ideals and in part on setting goals for the organization.

- People have many opportunities for *interaction* to foster dialogue and facilitate leadership initiatives or to provide understanding of the business and respect toward fellow workers' contributions and responsibilities.

- Different forms of learning opportunities support people's desire for their own *personal growth*.

It seems that these principles greatly benefit the older person in the ever more multigenerational workplace of the future. Taking ownership, heeding one's values, being part of a close-knit work team, and having the opportunity to learn summarize well the major characteristics of a modern workplace geared toward older workers.

Reversing Personal Curtailment

Rather than being viewed as a period of withdrawal, old age can be seen as a period of expanded productivity, joy, and accomplishment. Many older executives and business owners find this to be the most creative and exciting period of their working lives. Many retirees experience that same joy working in new and challenging fields. This notion of expanded mental capabilities and usefulness with age may well be the next great social movement in our society.

Self-Management and Expanded Personal Responsibility

Older people are increasingly finding that "if it's to be, it's up to me." This grasping of individual responsibility and declining reliance on institutions and organizations is a relatively new phenomenon in our general population. Self-assertion and taking personal responsibility seem to be a delayed reaction to the newfound independence inherent in a secure retirement income. Democratization of comfortable leisure, or at least the freedom to work at what you want, is creating a new social class that can, and wants to, contribute to society.

Public Contribution by the New "Leisure Classes"

Just as with earlier "leisure classes," many older people want to develop and use their talents productively, but not just to earn more income. For example, some enjoy the role of elder statesman, mentor, or ombudsman in the companies that employ them. A sense of mature responsibility is sure to grow in the decades ahead. We need effective general education to release the potential inherent in these emerging citizen-philosophers who do care what happens to us.

THE REVOLUTION IS HERE

American society is in the throes of a major economic, social, and even political revolution—the equation of age rather than youth has turned our world upside down in a relatively short period of time. In only a generation or two, we have gone from a youth-focused society to one where the aged wield primary power—and their power is growing. Does this mean generational strife, as some predict? The answer clearly rests on how we manage this shift in power.

Management implies directing effort to achieving some goal that has greater value than the energy, time, and resources expended to attain it. Whether we are managing a business, heading a university department, or directing the operations of a federal agency, the success of management is measured by the incremental changes in value. Therefore, when discussing the effective productivity of older employees, individually or collectively, the major question is how to avoid the pitfalls of a multigenerational society and how to make the organizational mixture of young and old successful.

The answer to that question will affect each of us for decades to come. It will have a great influence on our gross national wealth, our level of international competitiveness, and the quality of work life for workers of all ages and even the possibility of some intergenerational strife. This last point is critical. As the pool of younger workers shrinks and the economic burden of a ballooning older population falls more heavily on fewer and fewer shoulders, as, for example, with Social Security, the potential for conflict increases.

In a very real sense, however, our older workers are a key national asset, more vital to our future than oil or farmland or factories. Further, this is a workforce issue and a human productivity issue that includes everyone old enough to work and even many retirees who are still productive and contributing to our economy. Foremost, the effectiveness of our management of older people and their level and type of contribution is, or should be, a public issue of concern to everyone, because it affects everyone. Whether we encourage older people to remain in the workforce or push them out, as we sometimes have been doing, will have a great impact on the expected labor shortages of the new millennium and beyond. While in periods of economic downturn it is difficult to promote a retired person's need to work, people have needs in addition to income, and organizations have needs in addition to structured, 40-hour jobs. Flexibility in meeting the needs of all our people and organizations requires creative approaches. The good news is that there seems to be a substantial, pent-up demand for work by America's older citizens.

The American Association of Retired Persons reports that a substantial percent of its members 55 years of age or older regret having retired.[3] It is clear that millions of older Americans want at least some work to do. Yet, few U.S. companies allow workers to continue part-time employment while drawing part of their pension.

Advances in medical research, genetics, and pharmacology portend an exponential explosion in the numbers of people who will be healthy to a much later age in life. If we do not solve the problem of enabling people to work later if they desire, we may have a substantial population of restless, disaffected older people demanding changes in the way we do business. This could become an enormous social and economic problem.

Finally, since it has been assumed that much of the cost of supporting a growing retired population would have to be offset by increases in worker productivity, we must heavily draw on the special experience, knowledge, and abilities possessed in abundance by our older workforce. Research on older employees in recent years clearly indicates that our aging population can rise to the challenge if we manage our critical human resources more effectively. Few will escape the consequences of how well or poorly we manage older workers, not the newborn infant or the expiring octogenarian, for the issue involves our national health and wealth.

CHAPTER 2

The Demographic Imperatives

By 2012, the U.S. labor force will have grown to about 162 million people, an increase of 10% from today. But by then almost half of that total, about 77 million people, will be between 48 and 66 years old. It's the baby boomer generation, at that point already in, or on their way into, retirement age. Will they follow some of today's seniors' ideals, live in age-segregated retirement communities, and be totally leisure-oriented, consumerist, and part of a "nation of Florida"?

We don't really believe it. Over their lifetime, baby boomers have been active and fitness-prone, well educated and aware of their dominance in society. They were, indeed, a huge generational phenomenon. They were young and ambitious and, during times of economic strain, asserted their power, forcing the older generations into early retirement. They certainly contributed to some of the myths and misconceptions about "older workers." Now that they approach retirement age and have become "elderly," they produce significant shifts and distortions in the traditional workplace structure. This development is even more significant as they are followed by the "baby bust" generation, those born between 1968 and 1977, years with shrinking birthrates.

In the pages that follow, we review "a century of change," an analysis of the time period between 1950 and 2050, undertaken by the Bureau of

Labor Statistics (BLS) with surprising findings.[1] From there and narrowing our focus, we look at "the graying of the U.S. workforce," another analysis done by the BLS of the more immediate period ending in 2012.[2] Next, we deal with certain trends of employment and retirement of the "older worker" generation and review the situation of the Social Security system as well. Finally, we provide some international comparisons, as the aging of the population seems to be a global phenomenon.

Some of the key findings are unexpected and startling:

- At the end of this decade, the age group of the 55-to-64-year-olds will be at almost 20% of the labor force. In other words, one in every five employees will belong to the group of "older workers."
- At the same time and at peak periods of the U.S. economy, we may see certain labor shortages, which may require raising the labor participation rate of "older workers." In the age group of the 55-to-64-year-olds, the rate traditionally has been around 60 to 65%, or two in every three people. It may even be necessary to get some of the 65-and-older workers back into active roles, be it part- or full-time. In that age group, labor participation is down to 16%, or one in every six people.
- The aging of the labor force is a global phenomenon, albeit aggravated in the United States by the baby boomer situation. Higher life expectancy and declining labor participation rates among "older workers" produce disastrous effects on worldwide pension systems.

Let's now look at some of the detailed analyses.

A CENTURY OF CHANGE: THE U.S. LABOR FORCE, 1950–2050

In the May 2002 issue of *Monthly Labor Review*, the BLS published under this very appropriate title a profound analysis of the transformations that have occurred and will continue to occur in the U.S. labor force. There are several key findings that we want to highlight.

First, it appears that the growth of the labor force will slow significantly as we progress through the decades ahead of us. As we know, the baby boomers created remarkable growth rates of over 2% per year in the 1960s to 1980s. This led to an average annual growth of 1.6% for the labor force during 1950 and 2000. However, as the baby boomers start reaching retirement age and as the effects of the subsequent "baby bust" impact the overall numbers, the annual growth of the labor force in the years 2000 to 2050 is projected to slow down to an average 0.6% per year. While the first decade will still show growth of about 1.1% per year, the growth rate will drop subsequently to about 0.4% per year. These developments are expected to put significant strain on the availability of labor.

Second, dramatic changes are projected for the age structure of the labor force. We mentioned already that the baby boomers, the 77 million-strong generations born between 1946 and 1964, will reach the early retirement age set by the Social Security system by 2008. Its bulging ranks will make the age group of the 55-to-64-year-olds, or the "older workers," swell from 13% of the labor force in 2000 to 20% by 2020 and stay at that level for the following decades.

Similarly and with ever higher life expectancy, the age group 65 and older is projected to increase from 15.6% in 2000 to about 24.4% in 2050. In this age group people tend to retire, and labor participation rates fall. With all these changes, the ratio of people at work who make contributions to Social Security, to those in retirement who collect benefits, will decrease from about 3:1 today to 2:1 by 2030. The consequences to Social Security are obvious and well known.

Let's just pause here for a moment and try to digest and interpret the data. Many of the dramatic changes we heard about stem from the impact of the baby boomer generation as it moves onward in age. The ranks of "older workers"—the 55-to-64-year-olds—are swelling, as are those 65 and older as well, with many or most of them in retirement. Our country will be faced with two important challenges over the next 10 to 20 years:

1. *Possible labor shortage.* With shrinking growth in the labor force and ever increasing retirement ranks, the prospect of labor shortages is a real possibility. While the BLS sees immigration and outsourcing to foreign countries as ways to compensate for the slack, we suggest that a renewed focus on "older workers," including those in the 65-and-older category, might be a better solution to the problem. It will also help to offset the second challenge.

2. *Social Security*. While the need to shore up ailing pension systems seems to be a global challenge, the U.S. situation may warrant a slightly different approach. When the Social Security legislation was first enacted, median life expectancy was about 77 years. Now it's 82 years and will be 87 years by 2050. As people get older, it may be well to encourage greater numbers of "older workers" to stay at the active side of the labor pool—be it full- or part-time—and with that help to elevate the ratio of workers to recipients of benefits to a more reasonable level.

Returning to other findings of the analysis, it acknowledges major changes in the gender structure of the labor force. The share of women in the labor force grew from 30% in 1950 to almost 47% in 2000 and is expected to reach about 48%, or about half of the labor force, in 2050.

More importantly, the racial and ethnic composition of the labor force has changed and is projected to change further, as evidenced by these numbers:

	2000	2050
Whites, non-Hispanic	73%	53%
Hispanics	11%	23%
Blacks	12%	14%
Asians	5%	10%

Immigration has been a major source of this growing diversity. Immigrants tend to be in younger age groups and to show higher labor participation rates.

Let's now take a look at the more immediate labor force situation in the years ahead of us.

THE GRAYING OF THE U.S. WORKFORCE

In February 2004, the BLS devoted a whole issue of the *Monthly Labor Review* to labor force projections for the period 2002 to 2012. After our excursion into the larger, century-long analysis of the labor market, this will help narrow our focus to the more immediate situation ahead of us.

The economic assumptions for the period 2002 to 2012 project economic growth (gross domestic product—GDP) of 3% per year, based on productivity increases of 2.1% per year and annual growth of the labor force of 1.1%. This still relatively comfortable growth rate is expected to drop to 0.4% per year in the following decade, due to the retirement of the baby boomers, who will be at the age of 48 to 66 years by 2012.

The decade of 2002 to 2012 sees two countermoving developments in the labor force. The age group of older workers, the 55-to-64-year-olds, will grow by about 11 million, or 46%, to a total of 31 million, or 19.1% of the workforce. At the same time and due to the reduced birthrates of the "baby bust" generation that will be at age 35 to 44 by 2012, this age group will decline by 3.8 million, or 1%. The median age of the labor force in 2012 is projected to be the highest ever recorded, with 41.4 years.

In summary, the findings corroborate our earlier conclusions that a careful and deliberate focus on "older workers" is needed already during this first decade of the twenty-first century, in order to deal with the challenges posed by possible labor shortages and declining labor participation rates of the upper age groups.

In this context, it is interesting to look at some of the BLS' projections for certain occupations, which already today have a higher than the average 14% share of employees age 55 and older, with a tendency to increase further.[3] Among these occupations are:

	Share in 2002	Rate of increase to 2012
Sales & service representatives	31.2%	24.3%
Social workers	30.1%	26.7%
Systems analysts	27.3%	57.0%
Pilots & flight engineers	26.7%	17.8%
Market researchers	25.4%	24.7%
Special education teachers	23.7%	30.0%
Human resources, training & labor relations	23.0%	27.7%
Personal & home care aides	21.0%	40.5%

To reinforce some of our earlier comments, the BLS projects a labor force of 162.3 million by 2012, estimating the total of available jobs for the same time to be at 165.3 million. While the difference does not necessarily signal an immediate labor shortage—because other factors like immigration, multiple job holdings, and outsourcing need to be considered—it highlights the importance of a renewed focus on the almost 20% of "older workers" in the labor force.

EMPLOYMENT AND RETIREMENT TRENDS, SOCIAL SECURITY

As we look at older workers' mind-set and societal values, an important indicator is their labor participation rate—the percentage of older people either working or looking for work. For better illustration, we refer to Exhibit 2.1, which provides labor participation rates for certain years from 1950 to 2000 as well as projections to 2050. Looking at the rates for men 65 and older, we see how labor participation steadily declined from about 46% in 1950 to almost 16% in 1990, which is evidence of the increased reliance on income from Social Security and from other retirement plans. The rate is expected to turn upward again after that, in part probably due to financial concerns after the dot.com fiasco, but maybe also to account for a different mental attitude of the baby boomer generation.

In the age group of 55-to-64-year-old men, rates have stabilized since 1990 at a point where only two in every three men are working. On the women's side, labor participation is generally on the increase, and the "older workers" category is no exception. An important factor here is the possibility to collect Social Security benefits at age 62, which is an opportunity for many people to start enjoying leisure and recreation.

All in all, we may be seeing some reversal in these trends with raising the full retirement age to 67 years for Social Security recipients; with replacing many of the "defined-benefit" retirement plans with age-neutral "defined-contribution" ones; and with focusing more closely on "older workers" in view of the coming-of-age and early retirement of the first wave of baby boomers.

At this point, some comments on the situation of the Social Security system may be in order.[4] Traditionally, Social Security has been a pay-as-you-go system, and so far receipts have been higher than payouts, which has helped to build a $1.5 trillion trust fund for future spending. There is little doubt, however, about the impending problems.

With the retirement of the baby boomers and the overall increases in life expectancy, it is expected that the Social Security system will start using the trust fund in 2028 and that the system will run out of funds by 2042. As to possible solutions, a host of proposals is being debated, from raising payroll taxes as well as the "cap" for them, to raising full retirement age again, indexing the full retirement threshold to life expectancy, and allowing participants to channel some of the payroll taxes into private accounts with the potential for higher returns. One outcome seems clear: to avoid bankruptcy of the system, Social Security as we know it today will have to change.

As we see next, the situation in the rest of the world is not any better.

THE INTERNATIONAL PICTURE

We have analyzed certain data from the Organization for Economic Cooperation and Development (OECD), which includes data for European as well as Asian industrial nations.[5] The OECD seems well equipped in the research of international employment data. It is interesting to witness similar problems in the OECD area as we see them in the United States. In a recent study on "Ageing Societies and the Looming Pension Crisis," OECD has started focusing on the need of most member countries to reform their pension systems.

The reasons for the problem in OECD member countries, however, are somewhat different, allowing for other solutions as well. In Europe, due to persistent unemployment levels, the solution to that particular problem has often been to encourage older workers to retire early based on disability, long-term sickness, or unemployment. This reduced the unemployment numbers but led to surprisingly low

EXHIBIT 2.1: Civilian labor force participation rates by sex and age, 1950–2000 and projected, 2010–50

Group	1950	1960	1970	1980	1990	2000	2010	2015	2020	2030	2040	2050
Percent												
Total, 16 years and older	59.2	59.4	60.4	63.8	66.4	67.2	67.5	66.8	65.1	62.3	61.6	61.5
16 to 24	59.9	56.4	59.8	68.1	67.3	65.9	66.5	67.1	66.5	66.0	65.9	65.5
25 to 34	63.5	65.4	69.7	79.9	83.6	84.8	87.1	88.0	87.9	87.6	87.4	87.3
35 to 44	67.5	69.4	73.1	80.0	85.2	84.8	86.0	86.6	86.5	86.4	86.3	86.2
45 to 54	66.4	72.2	73.5	74.9	80.7	82.6	83.8	84.1	84.0	83.9	83.7	83.4
55 to 64	56.7	60.9	61.8	55.7	55.9	59.2	60.9	61.6	60.8	60.1	60.7	60.3
65 and older	26.7	20.8	17.0	12.5	11.8	12.8	14.8	16.2	16.3	15.2	13.3	13.4
Men	86.4	83.3	79.7	77.4	76.1	74.7	73.2	71.9	70.3	67.6	67.0	66.8
16 to 24	77.3	71.7	69.4	74.4	71.5	68.6	67.9	68.2	67.6	67.2	67.3	67.0
25 to 34	96.0	97.5	96.4	95.2	94.2	93.4	93.1	93.0	93.0	93.0	92.9	93.0
35 to 44	97.6	97.7	96.8	95.5	94.4	92.6	92.3	92.2	92.2	92.1	92.1	92.1
45 to 54	95.8	95.7	94.3	91.2	90.7	88.6	87.8	87.3	87.3	87.3	87.1	87.1
55 to 64	86.9	87.3	83.0	72.1	67.7	67.3	67.0	66.8	66.1	65.7	66.5	66.2
65 and older	45.8	33.1	26.8	19.0	16.4	17.5	19.5	21.0	21.0	19.6	17.3	17.3
Women	33.9	37.7	43.3	51.5	57.5	60.2	62.2	62.1	60.3	57.4	56.7	56.6
16 to 24	43.9	42.8	51.3	61.9	63.1	63.2	65.1	66.1	65.4	64.8	64.6	64.0
25 to 34	34.0	36.0	45.0	65.5	73.6	76.3	81.4	83.3	83.0	82.4	82.1	81.9
35 to 44	39.1	43.4	51.1	65.5	76.5	77.3	80.0	81.2	81.1	81.0	80.7	80.5
45 to 54	37.9	49.9	54.4	59.9	71.2	76.8	80.0	81.1	80.8	80.7	80.4	79.9
55 to 64	27.0	37.2	43.0	41.3	45.3	51.8	55.2	56.7	55.8	54.9	55.3	54.7
65 and older	9.7	10.8	9.7	8.1	8.7	9.4	11.1	12.5	12.6	11.7	10.1	10.1
White	—	—	—	64.1	66.8	67.4	67.6	66.8	65.0	62.1	61.5	61.4
Black	—	—	—	61.0	63.3	65.8	67.1	66.6	65.0	62.1	60.9	59.8
Asian and other[1]	—	—	—	64.6	65.4	66.5	67.5	67.4	66.4	64.9	64.2	64.9
Hispanic origin	—	—	—	64.0	67.0	68.6	69.0	69.1	67.9	65.8	64.6	63.8
Other than Hispanic origin	—	—	63.7	66.3	67.0	67.3	66.5	64.6	61.6	60.9	60.9	—
White non-Hispanic	—	—	—	64.0	66.8	67.2	67.3	66.4	64.4	61.1	60.5	60.5
Age of baby-boom generation	0–4	0–14	6–24	16–34	26–44	36–54	46–64	51–69	56–74	66–84	76–94	86–104
Difference between Men's and Women's Labor Force Participation Rates												
Total, 16 years and older	52.5	45.6	36.3	25.9	18.6	14.5	11.0	9.8	10.0	10.1	10.2	10.2
16 to 24	33.4	28.8	18.1	12.5	8.4	5.4	2.8	2.0	2.2	2.4	2.7	3.0
25 to 34	62.0	61.5	51.4	29.7	20.5	17.0	11.7	9.8	10.0	10.6	10.8	11.1

35 to 44	58.5	54.3	45.7	30.0	18.0	15.4	12.3	10.9	11.1	11.1	11.5	11.5
45 to 54	57.9	45.8	39.9	31.3	19.5	11.8	7.8	6.2	6.4	6.6	6.7	7.1
55 to 64	59.9	50.1	39.9	30.8	22.4	15.5	11.7	10.1	10.2	10.8	11.2	11.5
65 and older	36.1	22.3	17.1	10.9	7.7	8.1	8.4	8.5	8.5	8.0	7.2	7.3

Change (percentage points)

	1950–60	1960–70	1970–80	1980–90	1990–2000	2000–10	2010–15	2015–20	2020–30	2030–40	2040–50
Total, 16 years and older	.2	1.0	3.4	2.6	.8	.3	-.7	-1.8	-2.8	-.7	-.1
16 to 24	-3.5	3.4	8.2	-.8	-1.4	.6	.6	-.6	-.3	.0	-.4
25 to 34	1.9	4.3	10.2	3.7	1.0	2.5	.9	-.2	-.3	-.2	-.1
35 to 44	1.9	3.7	6.9	5.2	-.4	1.1	.6	-.1	-.1	-.2	.0
45 to 54	5.8	1.3	1.4	5.8	1.8	1.2	.3	-.2	.0	-.3	-.2
55 to 64	4.2	.9	-6.1	.2	3.3	1.7	.7	-.8	-.7	.6	-.4
65 and older	-5.9	-3.8	-4.4	-.7	1.0	1.9	1.5	.1	-1.1	-1.9	.0
Men											
16 to 24	-3.1	-3.6	-2.3	-1.3	-1.4	-1.5	-1.3	-1.6	-2.7	-.6	-.1
25 to 34	-5.6	-2.2	5.0	-2.9	-2.9	-.7	.2	-.5	-.5	.1	-.3
35 to 44	1.5	-1.1	-1.2	-1.0	-.8	-.3	-.1	-.1	.0	-.1	.0
45 to 54	.1	-.9	-1.4	-1.0	-1.8	-.3	-.1	.0	-.1	.0	.0
55 to 64	-.1	-1.4	-3.1	-.5	-2.1	-.8	-.5	-.1	.0	-.2	.0
65 and older	-12.7	-4.3	-10.8	-4.4	-.4	-.3	-.2	-.7	-.4	.8	-.3
Women											
16 to 24	3.8	5.6	8.1	6.0	2.7	2.0	1.0	.0	-2.8	-.7	-.2
25 to 34	-1.1	8.5	10.6	1.2	.1	1.9	1.9	-.7	-.7	-.2	-.6
35 to 44	2.0	9.0	20.5	8.2	2.7	5.1	1.3	-.3	-.6	-.3	-.3
45 to 54	4.3	7.7	14.4	11.0	.8	2.7	1.1	-.1	-.1	-.3	-.1
55 to 64	12.0	4.5	5.5	11.3	5.6	3.2	1.5	-.2	-.1	-.3	-.4
65 and older	10.2	5.8	-1.7	4.0	6.5	3.5	1.4	-.9	-.9	.4	-.6
White	—	—	—	2.8	.6	.2	-.7	-1.9	-2.9	-1.6	.0
Black	—	—	—	2.4	2.5	1.2	-.4	-1.6	-2.9	-.6	-1.1
Asian and other[1]	—	—	—	.8	1.1	1.0	-.1	-1.0	-1.5	-.7	.7
Hispanic origin	—	—	—	2.9	1.6	.4	.1	-1.2	-2.0	-1.2	-.8
Other than Hispanic origin	—	—	—	2.6	.7	.3	-.8	-1.9	-3.0	-.7	.0
White non-Hispanic	—	—	—	2.8	.4	.1	-.9	-2.0	-3.3	-.6	.1

[1]The "Asian and other" group includes (1) Asians and Pacific Islanders and (2) American Indians and Alaska Natives. Historical data are derived by subtracting "black" from the "black and other" group; projections are made directly, not by subtraction.

Note: Dash indicates data not available.

Source: "Labor Force Change, 1950–2050," *Monthly Labor Review* (May 2002), U.S. Bureau of Labor Statistics.

labor participation rates for 2001 in the age group of the 55-to-64-year-olds:

United States	60.2%
Japan	65.8%
UK	54.0%
Germany	41.5%
France	38.8%
Italy	19.4%

Therefore, OECD suggested to their member states, as a first step, to eliminate many of the provisions that induce early retirement. This would help increase labor participation rates and overall employment in the "older workers" age group. However, in order to be successful, stated the OECD report, "enterprises must learn to view older workers as a genuine asset" and change business attitudes, providing valid employment opportunities.

The OECD's observation is coming at the right time, and this is what our book is about. The "older workers" represent a wealth of experience, perspective, and wisdom that can be used to the great benefit of organizations that are willing to consider them a genuine asset and to invest in keeping them active and involved.

Let's briefly review the most important demographic developments:

• By 2012 the U.S. labor force will have grown to about 162 million people. Of those, about 77 million will be between 48 and 66 years old.

• The annual growth of the U.S. labor force will slow from a rate of over 2% in the 1960s to 1980s to about 1.1% in the first decade of the twenty-first century and to about 0.4 % thereafter, putting significant strain on the labor market.

- Already today, certain professions show an above-average share of workers aged 55 and older, projecting further significant increases for the future:

Social workers:	share of 30%, increasing 27% per year
Systems analysts:	share of 27%, increasing 57% per year
Special education teachers:	share of 24%, increasing 30% per year
Home care aides:	share of 21%, increasing 41% per year

- The percentage of men retiring has significantly increased since the 1950s

  in the group of 55-to-64-year-olds: from 13% to 33%
  in the group 65 years and older: from 54% to 82%

  With the expectation of certain shortages in the labor force and the need for qualified people, these trends may have to be reversed.

- While in the United States the avalanche of baby boomers has aggravated the general problem of higher life expectancy, the international situation is somewhat different. Particularly in Europe, the problem of high unemployment has led to incentives for early retirement, which now may have to be reversed. In the group of 55-to-64-year-olds, the percentage of people in retirement reached 59% in Germany, 61% in France, and 81% in Italy, compared to 40% in the United States (including men and women).

CHAPTER 3

The Evolving Meaning of Retirement

In human society, the concept of retirement is quite a recent development. In the gathering and hunting communities that first roamed the earth, it was imperative that everyone able to do so help provide the food, clothing, and shelter that sustained them. A person's role might shift from hunter of game to collecting berries or tanning the hides for clothing, but—as we can see today in such few of those cultures that still exist—the right to "earned idleness" would have been inconceivable. Life was too stark and demanding for that. Anyway, most folks didn't live long enough to retire even if that had been possible.

As societies evolved and grew into larger entities such as clans and tribes, and as technology improved, creating a wider range of useful skills, older people continued to be of service as counselors, teachers of the young, and teller of legends and stories. Some older people, men and women, over time became more valued.

Very gradually, as settled communities began to emerge, social hierarchy started to develop, leading in time to such notions as the rise of nobility. People would take care of their children's future and make it more likely that the children would return the favor. This meant in many cultures the concept of land-ownership and of concentration of wealth, with the emergence of the possibility of leaving an inheritance.

This era also saw the appearance of the classic professions of law, theology, and medicine, and, with that, corollary activities such as management, finance, and government emerged as well. With these more complex sets of tasks that required specialized knowledge, retirement—leaving such chores behind one—became more common. Yet most folks still could not comprehend the idea of retirement (idleness) even if they then lived with, and off, their children later in life.

Until the Industrial Age, the possibility and existence of a pension were not widely known. Early pensions were often a form of gratuity offered for faithful service such as time in the military. In most families people lived at just a notch above survival (as still is true in much of the world today), considering that to have food, clothing, and shelter was to be the most they could hope for.

In the United States, farmers—in our then dominantly agrarian society—tended to have large families to help with the farm and to possibly take care of parents when they got too old to work the land. Hence, offspring became the social security net. In urban areas, those at the bottom of the economic ladder depended on the toils of whatever work they could find. In our country, the needs of old age were most commonly met through personal savings—including individual annuities and insurance—as well as by some private pensions and certain government-sponsored programs. The term "pension" came to mean any periodic retirement income benefit.

Thus, a pension plan came to mean any program set up by an employer, labor organization, or government that provided regular income payments to retired persons meeting specific conditions set forth in the plan. Usually, a person might "withdraw" from active employment based on any number of reasons such as old age, disability, or death. Therefore, the primary topic to discuss here is the old-age form of pension.

The evolution of our industrial society has broadened and stimulated the growth of private and government pension programs. While, in an agricultural economy, tasks tended to be quite simple and straightforward, industrial-era jobs hinged on one's physical dexterity, on skills and experience, and on mental alertness. These requirements increasingly started to limit the age at which some people could function effectively. Hence, there have been increasing interest in, and demand for, old-age pensions, particularly in Western societies.

Formal pension systems covering significant portions of a given country's population began in the last quarter of the nineteenth century. Germany established the first truly national program in the 1880s. In the United States, that did not happen until 1935. In the private sector, the American Express Company created a first company-wide pension plan in 1875. During the next half century, approximately 400 more programs were established, primarily in the railroad, banking, and public utility fields. Similar developments in the manufacturing sector were slow to arrive because workers tended to be younger and often did not acquire tenure at the same rate as older employees.

All of the foregoing has been offered to make the point that there was nothing inherent in society in terms of the workforce receiving and being covered by pensions despite the rising need. Also when the Social Security system was established in the United States—much out of a sense of moral responsibility—the initial plans were quite limited as to coverage. Much later that coverage was extended and enlarged.

Current discussions about Social Security, pensions, and job security after a wave of downsizing and restructuring of organizations, after the impact of globalization and the rise of new organizational cultures, only highlight the notion that issues of retirement and how one experiences it are far from settled.

THE DEEPER MEANING OF RETIREMENT

The creation of the Social Security system in the United States was not an isolated event. During that same period, there were also enacted several related pieces of legislation, including the establishment of a minimum wage, of the 40-hour workweek—with overtime pay for time beyond that—and the emphasis on third-party venues to settle labor–management disputes. Many of those revolutionary developments have become the source of contentious debate ever since and often led to new laws. Many of these conflicts will be with us for some time to come.

The problem of many industrial jobs migrating overseas opened a new chapter of knowledge work and Information Age jobs at home. The increasing focus on new corporate cultures, on intellectual capital and self-managed forms of work, provides new and different challenges and opportunities to retirees who wish to continue some kind of engagement with the working world.

Ironically and sometimes tragically, in the 1940s, 1950s, and often well into the 1960s and 1970s, our nation was faced with a substantial retiring population who had little experience with leisure or its challenges. That early period abounded with stories of (primarily) men used to working 60 to 70 hours a week taking to a rocking chair on the front porch and dying soon thereafter from "underwork."

With that type of six-day workweek, quite a few, mostly industrial workers, often with low levels of education and no time to develop outside interests or hobbies, with limited social and media contacts, simply did not have any idea what to do with themselves. However, as leisure time, vacations, and media contacts—radio, television, and now the Internet—became more frequent, many older people had to face the question, How do I want to spend the rest of my life after no longer filling my time with work?

Don and Christine are a married couple in their mid-50s who retired on a full pension from the U.S. government. In their last few years before their retirement, they could, and often did, tell us exactly the number of years, months, days, and hours of how far away retirement was. Don was more relaxed about it but had a longing to be free of his supervisory responsibilities. Yet shortly after the magic date of their actual retirement, Christine was doing volunteer work in her community a couple of days per week, and Don was busy helping out at the local hospital. Neither of them had ironclad schedules for the volunteer efforts, which enabled them to travel and visit family and friends far from home when it suited their purposes. Their combined retirement income offered them many lifestyle options to suit their individual tastes but allowed them to contribute to society as well.

Christine and Don are probably close to the midpoint between retirees who can't even afford the medicines they need to take to maintain their health and those who own multiple residences, travel freely about the world, and contribute to—and sometimes assist—fund-raisers for worthy causes. Yet retirement has a personal meaning for each person along the spectrum.

RECENT AND FUTURE TRENDS

The passage of the GI Bill of Rights at the end of World War II and its continued availability to military personnel blew the lid off the creeping rise in this country's education and training that had characterized the previous century and a half. The previous notion of "terminal education"—the idea that the level of grade school education should be sufficient to match the needs of the increasingly complex workplace—is no longer adequate. The need for purposeful, lifelong learning has been replacing it.

Not only are the emerging workers of today better educated, more skilled, and more versatile than ever before, but there are strong indications that these trends will continue to develop during the coming decades. This trend toward greater intellectual involvement by workers is being matched by their increased physical prowess until far later in life. This trend seems to be virtually open-ended and even expanding. The increasing ability for older workers to contribute to (or even create) new enterprises as well as improving existing ones is phenomenal. A rapidly increasing number of people are becoming itinerant and/or contingent workers because that is what they want, and regular employers increasingly need such assistance.

To make this trend more pervasive and valuable to both workers and employers, we need at least the following seven factors to evolve:

1. Keep mentally, spiritually, and physically fit.
2. Develop more flexible organizational cultures.
3. Explore more fully our human diversity.
4. Encourage a culture of lifelong learning.
5. Interpersonal and group-creative synergies will be increasingly important and valuable.
6. Multiple and varied careers must be seen as an asset.
7. Possible conflicts between old and young need to be addressed.

Keep Mentally, Spiritually, and Physically Fit

If we think of ourselves as an amalgam of these three components that make us human, we need to recognize a need to balance and develop all in equal measure. In the last half century we have seen great progress in the ways to develop all three. Advances in our knowledge, know-how, and experience have made older people increasingly valuable as they get on in age rather than less so as in previous generations. Advances in meditative techniques have become widely available to all (perhaps with a little searching) to calm our minds, relax our bodies, and release our creative subconscious. Lastly, advances in medicine, in both treatments and general knowledge, have led to older people (real and potential) living longer, better, and more productively.

In the 1960s, we began to see an increasingly large number of older people walking or jogging for exercise. Today, the pursuit of lifelong learning is the maturing stage of such practices, and jogging one's mind is keeping it in shape.

Develop More Flexible Organizational Cultures

Specific jobs, assignments, and other characteristics of the Industrial Age organizations are becoming more flexible, fluid, and in some advanced organizations virtually obsolete. Assembling special teams to solve problems; to develop production or service innovations; and to implement change is becoming increasingly common. The inclusion of special resource persons in these teams as consultants, trainers, or expert members often offers fresh perspectives on an issue.

Tolerance of significant differences between team members is no longer enough. Personal uniqueness needs to be increasingly sought out and included when searching for answers. Members ought to try to make everyone a star by helping them to build up their success and contribution rates. The above may require considerable training and development of interpersonal skills but can position their organization for unusual success.

Explore More Fully Our Human Diversity

Some years ago, many business organizations started to use the Myers-Briggs Personality Profile as well as Preferred Learning Styles Analysis to help their personnel understand each other better. All too often, though, the tools were treated superficially rather than as a viable indicator for team integration and cooperation. Consequently, most such efforts suffered the fate of fads and quickly disappeared. Yet many of these tools offer much for understanding ourselves, for team building, and for interpersonal idea building and cooperation.

Also, many emerging organizational needs involve working across cultures and through very short contacts with a variety of people— much more than most people have been used to in the past. Howard Gardner at Harvard University has written much about this, first in his description of seven flavors of genius[1] and more recently about how to understand, nurture, and utilize this great diversity in our organizations. As global "connectivity" becomes more common and necessary, those older workers who have cross-cultural experience and inclinations can become more valuable. Retirees often have the time and leisure to develop their interests in such diverse areas.

Encourage a Culture of Lifelong Learning

Some people claim they learn something new every day. While this may be true, what matters is its content value. Lifelong learning doesn't fill your mind with unneeded or useless facts but expands your consciousness to grapple successfully with new challenges. This is what makes older workers valuable to others and to themselves. Each of us and the world need their contributions.

With the blossoming of new ways to learn new things through online courses, Public Radio and Television, and employer-sponsored education efforts, rapid adaptation to new challenges will become a way of life for older people who want to remain active and engaged. The straight-line career path is less appealing for many, as they prefer to move on to new horizons. Unfortunately, these ideas and possibilities seem countercultural to many of the older workers' belief systems.

Yet we find that once they begin to explore the broader possibilities that life now offers, they are intrigued.

Interpersonal and Group-Creative Synergies Will Be Increasingly Important and Valuable

Innovation, entrepreneurship, and advanced technology will be the primary business needs for the coming decades, here and abroad. How well positioned to excel in that environment will the collective "we" fare in our part of global surroundings? Many of our dying Industrial Age managers, executives, and even workers did not even notice such considerations. We can still see the remnants of that culture wherever jobs have been lost in such areas as America's Rust Belt and not re-placed by something better.

When jobs are lost in a given area, the first and primary focused re-sponse should be replacing them with something more competitive and preparing displaced workers to fill Information Age jobs rather then maintaining them in the ones of the same dying variety. America in particular has tended to rely on special (and usually rare) geniuses such as Henry Ford, Andrew Carnegie, and Bill Gates to keep the country in the forefront of technology, new concepts, and advanced products. These types of innovators will continue to lead, but as the world and its needs become more complex, new social systems such as neural networks of inventors will be needed and are already starting to emerge. This work revolution is increasingly spearheaded by older workers with a broader vision and maturity, and well in the forefront of such developments.

Multiple and Varied Careers Must Be Seen as an Asset

During the Industrial Age "a rolling stone gathered no moss," "job hoppers could not be relied upon," and "the search for long-term secu-rity" was the be-all and end-all for generations of workers. Yet today, a person who has had multiple careers (even up to five in a lifetime) is increasingly seen as an asset. The breadth of experience, perspective, and insight so gained can be seen as an exceptional asset in many situations. Former physicians as senators and Senate leaders can serve as telling examples of the type of achievement and workplace asset we are talking about.

Also, this phenomenon will not have been caused by simple job loss, but as a logical and natural development based on the person's curiosity, search for challenge, and quest for personal achievement. If this is done with consideration of others' needs and desires as well, we can certainly build a better and more inclusive and democratic society. Doing this, organizational cultures built on fear and scarcity of opportunity will lose and be overcome.

Possible Conflicts Between Old and Young Need to Be Addressed

The ongoing debate about the future of Social Security, pension plans, and job opportunities all involve potential conflicts between older and younger workers and have done that for a long time. Yet this is no longer just about competition for scarce jobs. Work, job assignments, and other related matters of earning income are coming to the fore. This is where the older worker's participation becomes critical. Right now and for some years to come there is, and will be, a shortage of labor of many types and experience levels.

In many ways, a deeper issue that will count will be one of attitude and motivation, of inner self-content that a person brings to the work. Here is where the advantage of the older worker can often be paramount. This is where the evolving meaning of retirement will be critical. If a job or work is seen only as a scarce commodity to be fought over (as with two dogs and one bone), our mutual future will go backwards.

Yet if we see cooperation of all ages in our multigenerational society, based on a fruitful and creative dialogue where we build new and better opportunities for all, the evolution of retirement can be looked forward to with hope and promise.

CHAPTER 4

Shedding Common Assumptions, Myths, and Stereotypes about Older Employees

While the behavior of every age group is stereotyped by others to some degree, no group is as negatively affected by such generalizations as the elderly; at least other age groups are expected to outgrow their idiosyncrasies.

Older people are often perceived as poor, isolated, senile, unhappy, and unhealthy or as very well-off, playing endless golf into the sunset of their lives. As employees, they are often viewed as unmotivated and as less creative and less productive than younger workers. Under these assumptions, they don't seem to offer characteristics that lead to promotions or to selection for new learning opportunities.

Several studies have shown that managers sometimes engage in age discrimination without being aware of it. Years back, in 1977, a survey conducted of 1,570 subscribers to the *Harvard Business Review* sought to assess the degree to which age discrimination affected managerial decisions.[1] The respondents were divided into two groups, and each group was asked to evaluate a series of problems involving poor worker performance and decisions regarding training and promotions. The problems presented to the two groups were virtually identical except for the age of the employee involved in the incident. One-half dealt with a younger worker, and the other half with an older one.

In each of the situations, the older employee fared worse in the respondents' evaluations, regardless of the person's qualifications. When both an older and a younger worker were failing to adequately perform the job, the older employee was seen as resistant to change, and the respondents recommended reassignment. Those surveyed believed, however, that the younger worker could benefit from an "encouraging talk." Similarly, the older, equally qualified employee was perceived as less motivated to keep up with changing technology, as less creative, and as less able to deal with job-related stress. Age bias has been around for a long time.

What this and more recent research reflect is the self-fulfilling nature of discriminatory thinking. There is a tendency among some managers (as well as perhaps among many people in general) to believe that workers gradually lose their abilities as they age. Because advancement is usually based on the organization's view of the employee's potential, older workers are frequently not considered as candidates for such opportunities; rather, they may be seen as obstacles to the company's growth.

In many cases, the ideal candidate for a particular job is believed to be an individual in his or her 20s with a few years of work experience. Several studies suggest that many personnel specialists and managers have set their minds on this image and will not even consider an older worker who is better qualified and willing to accept the proffered salary. Moreover, having been raised in a society where "agism" is rampant, older employees all too often begin to act the part expected of them.

CULTURAL NOTIONS ABOUT AGE AND WORK

The mistaken notions about older people are so numerous and widespread that not all of them can be covered in a single chapter. Therefore, specific assumptions related to productivity, health, and learning are dealt with later. Here we explore eight of the more general concepts that many people perceive as characterizing aged employees and the negative impact of such generalizations on older people in the workplace:

1. Older people should retire to make way for younger employees.
2. Most older people are pretty much alike.

3. The basic job needs of older people in general are different from those of younger people.
4. As people age, they tend to focus on the past.
5. Most older employees cannot, or will not, change to meet the changing needs of the organization. They prefer to coast and shy away from promotions or challenge.
6. Age is a disease—a slow, but continuous, process that cannot be reversed.
7. Old age is (or should be) a period of relative calm and stability, and that's what older people want.
8. As people age, they become more critical, complaining, and suspicious.

These eight commonly held beliefs, gleaned from various publications of the National Council on Aging, lay an "apparently" rational foundation for grouping all older employees into a single bag that can be nicely labeled and put on a shelf without feelings of guilt.

Before examining the truth of such generalizations, consider their implications. Age discrimination often affects the older worker's self-image, employment status, and potential opportunities. Consequently, many older workers internalize society's biases toward them and behave in such a manner as to reinforce these myths. Hence, such myths and assumptions may create a self-fulfilling prophecy.

Older individuals suffer from depression to a much greater degree than younger people. Many of them believe that their level of competence will begin to slip further as they grow older.

Concrete results of agism are proven by older employees' reemployment rate, their potential income, and their chances for promotion. Unemployed workers over 45 can expect to wait at least four times as long for new jobs as workers under 20 years of age, according to one study. When they do finally find work, the job often will be lower-paying and carry less status than their original position.

Coser noted in a classic study that "educational level is not related in the same way to retirement intentions of men and women. Male prospective retirees tend to have less education than those not planning to retire, which is consistent with [their] occupational differences. However, female prospective retirees are likely to have more education than women who have no intention of retiring."[2] She explains this contradiction by examining occupational differences. "Men's educational level is usually matched by their occupation," and it is men in routine occupations who are more likely to retire, if they can afford to do so. "In contrast, women's educational level is usually not as well matched by the socio-economic level of their occupation. Women generally are [more] likely to have routine occupations and those who are better educated tend to be dissatisfied with the relatively low level of employment available to them" and therefore tend to retire earlier if they can afford to do so. This has largely been reversed in the last two decades, but there is still some way to go.

Finally, the situation regarding promotions for older workers can be dismal. For example, one manager in her 50s described her superior's consistently excellent evaluations of her performance. She was told she was one of the top three performers in her department and its strongest manager. In spite of this, "she was denied a promotion on the basis of the superior's *feelings* about her age rather than on the basis of her performance." It is no wonder, then, that the senior employee's output and attitude may deteriorate, leaving the organization to deal with a worker who has become a liability.

Some segments of society, in an attempt to cope with the growing number of retirees, have developed social and educational programs that build upon, and perpetuate, earlier activities and encourage the elderly to be self-centered and passive. Such programs often segregate older individuals from other age groups and focus on activities rather than the development of marketable skills.

In contrast, at least one author suggested a different orientation for older people: focusing on participation and self-actualization. He believed that the skills and abilities of older people are valuable and that they should "continue to participate in the mainstream of society because [they] . . . may help overcome some of the societal problems facing the nation."[3] This can be done through their mentoring of the young, volunteer work, and teaching special subjects.

None of this denies that aging sometimes creates problems for some individuals and possibly their organizations. Certainly, one does change as one grows older. The goal here is to separate myth from reality and "what counts" from that which "makes no difference."

Accordingly, we want to ask, What are some of the real problems that confront the elderly?

Aside from the physical changes that the older person experiences, the process of aging may also be characterized, to differing degrees, by loss and social disengagement. For those who opt to retire, there is frequently a financial loss and, perhaps, a loss of status and authority. There is often a change in living arrangements and community, caused either by the individual moving or by his or her children leaving the home or area where they all once resided. Finally, there may be the loss through death of one's spouse, contemporaries, siblings, or parents.

Myths that pervade this culture—such as that the elderly are poor, lonely, unhealthy, institutionalized—become realities only as a function of a given person's life history. Most older people live independent, socially active lives, with many being well above the poverty level (money worries are often a greater issue for younger people). Only a very small percentage of the elderly live in nursing homes or other institutions. Against this background, we can examine the specific stereotypes that are often used as justifications, either consciously or unconsciously, for discriminating against older workers.

Belief: Older Employees Should Retire Early and Make Way for Younger Employees

Aside from being a self-serving battle cry for some younger people, this belief clearly has wide currency among some top-level managers, human resource development professionals, and others concerned with the long-range health of the organization. Why else the push for early retirement even when such programs will cost the organization so much, long into the future?

Often buried in this cry are the assumptions that older people cannot contribute much to the future of the organization; that the future depends on the young; and that the needs of the young are more important than the needs of the elderly ("They've had their chance; now give us ours" is a common assumption of society). The general rationale of those who believe that the old should give way to the young is that the young have many more years to give to the organization; that they will eventually take over anyway; that they are inherently superior performers (because they are young and therefore full of energy and good ideas); and that they will grow discouraged and leave if their way upward is blocked. As we move from routine to knowledge work, this myth needs to be reappraised.

As turnover statistics indicate and although the young may have more years to give, they tend not to give them to their first or second employer. Also, turnover rates tend to be lower among older workers than among younger ones. There are also many questions about the young being inherently superior performers except in jobs requiring great strength and agility—a lessening work requirement today. Good (sound) ideas usually spring from the rearrangement of knowledge and experience in novel ways to solve current problems, and older employees tend to have an abundance of each.

In reality, some people do become less competent as they age, but much depends on what they are doing and whether the particular abilities that are declining are directly related to their job. The great number of executives, political leaders, and scientists who capably lead their organizations until they are well into their 80s or 90s shows the fallacy of assessing contribution on the basis of age. An executive who opts for early retirement at 55 may be contributing less than executives who strike their stride at 55 and continue their high performance rate into their 80s.

In some cases, an increasingly marginal employee might well be able to come up to employment standards with a change of job or assignment. Most people who enjoy reasonably good health can be useful and productive to the very end of their lives. They may even become more capable as they age. The notion that most people become less capable as they grow older is agism at its worst. The reality is that while some do decline, others become more able. We need to consider each case (person) individually. In the era of the Age Discrimination in Employment Act (ADEA), the penalty for not doing so has become substantial.

Two final points are pertinent here. First, much of this "make-way" viewpoint is based on the assumption that there are a limited number of jobs and if one person (presumably old) holds the job, another person (presumably younger) is denied the position. Also, we are all familiar with the depiction of the organization as a pyramid and the implied conclusion that there are fewer and fewer openings available as one moves toward the top. In some organizations, this is the case. But in the downsized and delayered organizations of the last few decades, with personal computers becoming more common, the opposite may be more true.

There is seldom, if ever, a fixed correlation between the number of jobs available and the ages of those who hold them. Our analysis of the demographics for the first decade of this century is proof of that. In addition, we have to consider that the job market contracts and expands as a function of general business conditions, entrepreneurial effort, government policy, and so on and is always in a state of flux. Simple, one-to-one-job thinking is erroneous, except possibly within a given organization. Even then, laying off an older worker would hardly guarantee that a younger person would get the job. Job requirements in most cases are far more complex than that.

Second, it has often been found that the jobs at the top of the organization are the hardest to fill. These positions require a breadth of experience, wisdom, and maturity seldom found in younger people. American companies have been set to encourage early retirement for years, and there is scant evidence that these actions have improved these organizations' performance. While some younger individuals may have gained, society is often paying a heavy price for this loss in effectiveness, gross national product, and taxable revenues. Setting older people aside in favor of younger ones can be very costly.

Belief: Most Older People Are Pretty Much Alike

The notion that older people are alike, which allows people to stereotype them, flies in the face of logic and common sense. In reality, we are most like one another when we are babies, because so little has happened to make us distinctive. As people grow, they acquire skills, knowledge, and experiences that set them apart from other individuals. Time also allows our genetic differences to manifest themselves; consequently, as we age, we become less, not more, like each other.

A study conducted of the elderly in northern California further establishes this point.[4] The researchers examined ten different lifestyles of 142 people born in the early 1900s. They discovered a great deal of diversity in the living and working arrangements of these individuals. Those who were financially secure were able to choose whether to retire or to continue working. The ability to choose, however, was considered an essential right by these individuals. Similarly, the selection of housing and leisure-time activities covered a broad spectrum. It is interesting to note that none of those surveyed said that they would opt to live in a "high-rise multiple-dwelling unit restricted to aged residents." The authors concluded that, as with any other age group, the needs of the elderly cannot be planned for in a "monolithic way." Because the psychological and physical well-being of older people varies immensely, it can no longer be assumed that the "package" approach—one type of health care, work, leisure-time activities, and housing arrangements—will satisfy the needs of all.

On the job, these differences also cry out for individual treatment. We should look at each person and his or her needs and abilities as unique. This need for individual differentiation among older workers is upsetting to some managers because it makes sweeping generalizations and blanket policies difficult to apply. It requires that we devote more personal attention to the differing needs of each employee. But if those needs are attended to, it also allows each employee's potential to be used by the organization to a greater extent.

Considerable research suggests that the production of innovative ideas is more a matter of personality and training than of age and that the source of the best ideas may not necessarily be restricted to the bright young person. Unfortunately, the habit of offering suggestions may have been wiped out of some older employees, and the challenge to many supervisors might be to tap into that unique reserve of know-how so that it can be successfully applied in a current context. Now that in many organizations certain layers of managers have been eliminated, new opportunities may be available, particularly in self-managed teams.

Belief: The Basic Job Needs of Older People in General Are Different from Those of Younger People

Despite the potential for ironic contradiction between this point and the last one, many people believe that the basic needs of old people are different from those of young ones. Yet people of all ages share the same needs for the basics of life—food, clothing, shelter, and good health. Equally important are the psychological requirements for security, love, companionship, belonging, self-respect, and the respect of others, as well as the need for recognition and achievement. These fundamental human needs are not lost with age and may actually increase for some individuals. While there are some obvious differences in specific needs, such as those related to the type and amount of health insurance coverage required, family needs and other obligations may be more important than age differences.

Where the needs of the various age groups have been shown to be different, it was not always to the elderly person's disadvantage. Of course, some of the needs of the elderly are different because of changes in their physical condition or situation. For instance, they generally require a different level of insurance coverage. Most older ladies do not need obstetrical coverage but would be interested in a greater amount of hospital insurance. Bodily changes also may create a need for some physical changes in the workplace as a particular older person may prefer a slower-paced and less stressful job. None of these differences, however, are sufficient to justify society's transformation of the elderly into a subspecies possessing lowered lifestyle expectations.

Belief: As People Age, They Tend to Focus on the Past

The statement that the elderly "live in the past" ties in with other stereotypes of them as out of touch and, perhaps more significantly, out of reach. Focusing on the past is considered by many people as synonymous with senility. Instead, there is the theory that the process of life review or reminiscence serves a useful function of helping the individual to gain perspective on the meaning of his or her life. It has nothing to do with brain disease. As we learn in later chapters, this process of synthesizing past experiences allows the individual to approach new situations with a clearer understanding of how to handle them. Young people reminisce about high school or college days (or earlier), so reminiscing may well be a lifelong pattern for some people; but the young also have a lot less to reminisce about.

Belief: Most Older People Cannot Cope with Changes in the Organization

People's ability to handle change is related to how well they handle stress, their tolerance for ambiguity, and the value that they receive from the changes themselves. If a person has experienced job change as mostly negative, it should not be surprising that he or she views change as bad news and may resist it. This calls for greater and more reasoned explanation by management of the purpose behind the change and the nature of the change itself.

While a tolerance for ambiguity is important for nearly everyone, people also need to be able to make sense of what is going on about them. A sound, systematic plan for change, broadly understood and implemented in an orderly fashion, reduces ambiguity and the seeming chaos that all too often accompanies organizational change. Some younger people who might be action-oriented rather than contemplative might like the excitement of chaos. But someone who has had to make change work and who has suffered from poorly planned and implemented change may not be as enthusiastic. Also, when change is related to age differences, it often favors the young, so an older employee's reluctance may reflect only common sense.

Finally, prolonged or excessive stress over a number of years does lessen a person's physical capacity to be resilient, and older employees are less likely to be given stress-management training than younger people are because of the types of discrimination previously mentioned. Stress-management techniques, methods for visualizing end results, and meditative (relaxation) exercises can go a long way toward helping an older person manage change effectively.

In a later chapter, we also discuss the importance of learning as a means to heighten older people's flexibility and adaptability to change. Mastering new knowledge and different skills not only is a healthy motivational experience but translates into the ability to meet ever more difficult challenges. Learning refreshes the mind and helps the older person in particular to adjust to changing circumstances. Unfortunately, as was mentioned before, older employees are often prevented from participating in those kinds of learning experiences.

Belief: Aging Is a Disease—a Slow But Continuous Process That Cannot Be Reversed

At the outset, we have to reaffirm the common perception that today's elderly are much more vital and in better health and strength than the generations before them. Having said this, any discussion of an older person's physical or psychological well-being requires a consideration of that person's past to understand his or her current situation. While it is possible to isolate a time period in one's life for self-examination, it is impossible to do so without risking some distortion. As we all know, there are also some physical body changes that accompany the aging process. Vision and hearing acuity may diminish; the skin becomes less elastic; there may be degenerative changes in the joints and vascular changes that can affect the supply of blood to the heart and brain. Despite such changes, age is definitely *not* a disease. Aging is a process. The physical or mental problems that one confronts as one grows older are a function of many factors, for example, one's genetic makeup, socioeconomic class, diet, and amount of exercise, as well as simple aging and lifestyle.

Again, an important study on chronic health problems published some years ago included the observation that about two-thirds (67%) of those reporting chronic conditions indicated that those conditions did not interfere with their ability to remain active.[5] In addition, some people ignore the reality that several studies have found that many of those people with chronic health problems developed and experienced some of these conditions long before they could be classed as elderly. For instance, we should realize that diabetes is a chronic ailment, yet hundreds of thousands of afflicted employees of various ages carry out their daily work satisfactorily for decades, without this chronic ailment interfering with their output. Age, therefore, should not be considered synonymous with debilitating disease or pathology.

Belief: Old Age Should Be a Period of Calm and Stability

Many believe that older people can no longer handle the changing demands of the workplace. The belief that older people desire a quiet, reflective lifestyle may certainly be true in some cases. But this does not mean that *all or even most* wish to retire, as some claim when pushing for the early retirement of others. Many older employees have a need for stimulation, for an opportunity to use their imagination, and even for challenge. How else can they feel that life is interesting and rewarding? In fact, this is exactly why many people look forward to retirement. It is often seen as *freedom* and *opportunity*, the first chance in their working lives to escape monotony and boredom, to do something different. The belief that older people want to sit in a rocking chair and do nothing is largely an outdated model of reality carried over from a time when people had to suppress their thoughts and feelings in order to survive under autocratic and most often unimaginative management regimes.

Today, "quality managers" can make a person's job challenging and rewarding by the delegation of decision-making authority, the use of problem-solving task forces, or self-managed teams. The equitable distribution of varied and interesting assignments can make a great difference in any person's life. There is not much current reality in the belief that older people want repose above all.

Belief: As People Age, They Become More Critical, Complaining, and Suspicious

In most cases, these descriptors do not apply solely to the older individual. Research has found that, barring some debilitating disease, personality traits tend to remain stable across the adult life span. One study revealed that the elderly described themselves in nearly the same way as they had when they were younger.

This emphasizes, again, that aging is a process. Most physical and mental changes cannot simply be deemed reserved for old age. Rather, "context" is almost everything when one is attempting to understand and describe an individual's life status. However, if older employees are shunted aside in the workplace and their ideas and experience are discounted, as often happens, it should not be surprising that they become more critical, complaining, and suspicious of management and even of other employees who treat them poorly.

What does all this mean with respect to the adaptability of the older employee? Several studies found that there was little relationship between the age of top executives and a company's financial success. Specifically, they discovered that there was no statistically significant difference between the "sales, assets, net income, stockholders' equity, and number of employees, for companies whose top executive is over 65 years of age and those firms with younger top executives." This, one of the authors believes, supports the concept that "older top executives do not suffer a decline in intelligence or capability."[6] Another study included an examination of whether there is a relationship between the promotional expenditures of a company and the age of its management. The findings did not support the hypothesis that if managers grew more conservative as they aged, they would hesitate to spend large sums of money on advertising campaigns.

It would seem, then, that the older employee can adapt to changes in the workplace very well and in a manner that allows them to compete successfully. While many older people prefer to slow their work pace, this is a function of their specific needs. It does not, as we continue to emphasize, reflect the situation as a whole for *all* older individuals. What is essential for the elderly, as for any age group, is the possibility of pursuing whatever lifestyle and work situation best suit their needs and abilities.

FACTS AND FALLACIES ABOUT OLDER WORKERS' JOB ATTITUDES AND PERFORMANCE

Following is a series of additional questionable, but common, beliefs about older employees in the workplace. They add a special dimension to the negative additional sources of antiage biases. Here they are given with their countervailing reality.

Fallacy: Older people want to retire as soon as possible.

Fact: Some do. As a matter of fact, Bureau of Labor Statistics tables show that about one-third of the 55-to-64-year-olds retire early, probably lured by the possibility to start drawing Social Security benefits at age 62. In the 65-years-and-older group only 16% of the people continue working. However, several studies indicate that half of the retirees over age 55 would prefer to work and continue to use their job skills. This is consistent with other surveys that say that many would like to continue to work part-time and some to work at less strenuous or more interesting jobs.

Fallacy: Older workers are interested only in a progression from work to retirement.

Fact: Many older workers have been living what Ken Dychtwald and Joe Flower call a "linear life plan," by which people *learn* for 15 to 20 years, work for 30 to 40 years, rest for a while (retirement), and then die.[7] However, an increasing number, up to 30% by some estimates, start new careers after formally retiring on a pension and/or Social Security, go back to school, or seek out part-time work for as long as they are able.

Fallacy: Older people seek leisure and want to avoid responsibility.

Fact: Some older people may long for a life free of responsibility (perhaps we all do at times). But a survey conducted at two large companies found that more than 20% of their employees are caring for an elderly relative, in addition to their job responsibilities. Also, large numbers of older people are dedicating a great deal of their time and other resources to caring for children, grandchildren, and even great-grandchildren.

Fallacy: Older workers enjoy relatively high incomes and therefore are too expensive to keep on the payroll when younger employees could do the work for less.

Fact: Several studies show that, overall, older employees do not earn more than younger workers and that (depending on the employer), often at about age 50, real earnings begin to decline. The cost ratios most often favor older workers when a generous medical or retirement plan is involved—the medical plan being more important for lower-paid employees and the pension plan the greatest factor for higher-paid employees.

Fallacy: If layoffs were determined solely on the basis of performance, older employees would be hurt.

Fact: Grumman Corporation, for instance, at one time found that when it laid off workers on the basis of detailed performance evaluation, the average age of the workforce went *up* from 37 years to 45 years. There is considerable testimony in the literature that older workers are indeed very productive.

Fallacy: Younger employees discriminate most against older employees.

Fact: Most age discrimination in the workplace—in educational opportunities, in promotions, in changing job requirements—is based on decisions of managers who are mostly over 40. Younger managers often lack the power to set such a policy or to approve its implementation.

AN AGE FOR ACHIEVEMENT

Dispelling myths and stereotypes about age is not enough. We need a positive focus on age and the abilities that develop with age. We need to generate a positive self-fulfilling prophecy about aging, a prophecy of old age being potentially the most productive period of our lives, when all of our talents and development reach fruition. Age can be a period of expansion, fulfillment, and achievement for those who believe it and desire it.

A new age-related phenomenon has developed in the last half century—a host of people looking forward to the joys of retirement. But all too often, behind that joyous anticipation lurks the relief of going *away from* something—work, an onerous job, the controls and limitation of the workplace—rather than *toward* something positive. Old age should not be a burden; for many it is becoming a period when old dreams are rediscovered, dusted off, modified to reflect a greater sense of the world, and pursued with passion.

Don't we sometimes remember our mother saying with a wistful smile when we were very young: "Life begins at 40?" It's questionable that many people believed that at that time, but nonetheless, for many it proved true. Now that we are many decades past that crossover point, we realize that a fuller life began at 50 and has been picking up speed ever since.

Many of us have been told about the countless examples of high achievement and public service on the part of noteworthy individuals. Here are some examples:

- Konrad Adenauer was the first chancellor of the Federal Republic of Germany and remained in office until the age of 87.
- Irving Berlin was still working when he died at age 101.
- Alan Greenspan at almost 80 years of age is still heading the Federal Reserve.
- Former president George H. W. Bush celebrated his 75th birthday with a parachute jump from a military airplane.
- Hulda Crooks, who died at age 101 in 1997, started her career as a mountain climber when she was 66. She climbed Mount Whitney and repeated that achievement 23 times until she was 91 years old. At that high age, she also climbed Mount Fuji, the highest peak of Japan.

Is this burst of learning, skill development, personal growth, and contribution only for the exceptional? Not at all. There are also chief executive officers of major corporations, creative writers, artists, actors, and politicians whose careers have run into their 90s. Also, for each of these distinguished names, there are thousands of common older people doing exceptional and valuable work late in life, and their numbers are growing as more and more older people are "finding themselves" at last. Increasingly as we age, we need to create a healthy, positive image of ourselves, so that our abilities (despite possible problems) are continuously growing. This bounty can be harvested on the job by millions of people.

PART II

MANAGING—AND VALUING—OLDER WORKERS

At this point in our continuing journey, we review some of the enjoyable aspects of dealing with older workers—their experience, their mature and can-do attitude, and their motivation. We also examine how we create the right environment and culture to make them feel welcome and included; to enable them to grow and develop; and to provide them with opportunities for achievement.

Older employees will be an important faction of tomorrow's workforce—actually the fastest-growing age group of the Information Age labor force. Their talents and enthusiasm will help support and propel the economy. Therefore, we ought to make sure they receive the recognition and respect they deserve for their expertise and experience.

In the following pages, we address the many pertinent issues for the older employees' role in the workplace:

- *The value of experience* of older workers, in particular their ability to synthesize, to be creative, and to contribute to their work teams. We enhance this chapter with a case study on the Vita Needle Company, a seniors-only workplace, which gives us a *real-life perspective* on the work ethics and productivity of our senior citizens.

- *Successful safety, health, and wellness partnerships*, which is decisive in successfully managing an older workers' environment. The chapter focuses on some of the most common problems and, at the same time, provides detailed guidance on stay-well programs, so important for our seniors. In addition, it includes some recommendations for making older people's lifestyles healthier.

- *Training and education*, so important for the older worker, who depends on them for continued mental challenge and for being able to better adjust to changing circumstances. Again, we add here an *executive perspective*, a few interesting comments from a recent interview with AES Corporation's chief human resources officer Jay Kloosterboer.

- *Building motivation and morale*, a task not much different among older employees than among their younger peers. Motivation is always self-motivation, based primarily on professional challenge and opportunities for personal growth. Older people tend to be particularly sensitive to motivational issues because such issues help bring about a renewed purpose for their lives and support their personal well-being.

- Finally, *appraising older employee performance*, a thorough overview of the many sensitive aspects of age discrimination. As the chapter shows, this task is not difficult to handle if we manage fairly and treat the older employee the same as anyone else. Past wrongful practices, however, have led to certain preconceptions of some supervisors, who will need clear instructions and training to correct these behaviors. Once more, we include a *real-life perspective* on this particular topic, describing and summarizing the new Civilian Performance Appraisal System of the U.S. Coast Guard. It's a unique system and a good model, developed with active participation of many U.S. Coast Guard civilian employees, in a democratic approach not experienced before in this mostly command-and-control environment.

Older employees can, and increasingly will, be a true asset to organizations that understand to take advantage of their experience and expertise, their work ethics, and their motivation, as well as their stabilizing influence on today's multigenerational workplace.

CHAPTER 5

The Value of Experience

"Retirees have spent a lifetime developing their skills. Many of these individuals were highly productive up until the day they retired and they want to continue to create, connect and deliver value." This extraordinary and unequivocal statement, taken from the Web site of the recently founded service provider *YourEncore*, describes well the benefit of older workers.[1] *YourEncore* is recruiting retired, high-quality scientists and engineers for the needs of prospective companies like Eli Lilly, Boeing, and Procter & Gamble. "It's a new business model," confirms Alpheus Bingham, vice president of Eli Lilly, "that is leveraging current demographic trends to give us access to the talent we need from one of the most important and fastest growing segments of the knowledge workforce—retirees."

With the general aging of the workforce, employers have to respond in different ways to mature worker issues because talent shortages will be a major problem. Unfortunately, many companies still hold low opinions of older workers. "Yet we've found from research that the stereotyping is unfounded," says Diane Piktialis, senior product manager of personnel consultant company Ceridian. "Older workers can learn new technologies, and are less absent than younger workers."

FACTORS FAVORING OLDER EMPLOYEES

What kind of output can we expect from an older employee? While many still assume that the ability to produce declines with age, in many fields the opposite is true. If productivity is defined as the value of the work received for the resources expended, age may have little bearing on it. An experienced auto mechanic, age 68, may return many more times the value in marketable labor than his colleague, age 18 and just learning the trade, even taking into account wage differentials. Similarly, an older salesperson might well be able to outsell a younger competitor for reasons related to experience, know-how, and empathy, whereas in a job requiring considerable physical strength, a younger employee might have an edge.

What is the general productivity record of older employees? Where do we see their strengths and favorable work attributes? Where can management focus its attention for greater payoff from older workers?

Because of their greater experience, older employees usually have a more farsighted view of their work. Perhaps because they think that they cannot find a new job as easily as younger people can—and we know this is going to change—older workers tend to be more accommodating and responsible in their attitude toward work. In addition, if they have invested a number of years with an organization, they tend to be more loyal to the company and require fewer inducements to remain with it.

By the time workers reach their middle years, they have developed work habits that enable them to produce at a steady rate and to achieve consistent quality. Older workers also have some advantages with regard to accidents. Data from the U.S. Bureau of Labor Statistics have led to the conclusion that younger workers are hurt more often, but less seriously, than older employees.[2] The reason may be that, in the course of their work experience, older employees often develop techniques for avoiding accidents that younger workers have not mastered yet.

The older worker usually shines brightest when it comes to absenteeism and tardiness. Comparative studies have shown that a much higher percentage of older employees in the insurance sector had a perfect attendance record.

THE IMPACT OF NEW CORPORATE CULTURES

Since the middle of the twentieth century, we have seen more democratic, inclusive, and mature models of organizational cultures evolve and replace earlier, more hierarchic structures. Today, there are substantial openness, willingness to share feelings, ideas, and information, and a newfound flexibility in establishing a team environment. Leadership passes from person to person, depending on who has particular expertise and experience. People, while aware of their diverse backgrounds and ages, develop a sense of unity within their work group and appreciate the value of other people.

For the older worker this means a lot more acceptance and inclusion because of the change in personal and organizational relationships. Older people offer a wealth of talent and are often recognized as role models and mentors. For example, Kevin, a young man in his late teens, had dropped out of school and had a record of job-hopping when he was hired as a plumber's helper by a medium-sized contractor. He was assigned to work with John, an older and experienced plumber. He quickly noticed that John did not "put him down" as the other journeymen did to their assistants. John taught him many things about the work, with persistent and reliable attention to details. Kevin quickly noted that "John was the only lead man who did not 'rip off' the company by sitting in the truck drinking coffee half of the morning." Kevin soon developed a deep respect for John and his ways and in time came to emulate him and his work style.

Older workers greatly benefit from these new organizational models. In a self-managed environment, recognition by peers and teammates strengthens their self-esteem. Their pride in professional competence and the maturity of their values make them trusted in their relationships with others and well liked in their social interactions. Mutual achievement leads to abundant joy and fulfillment.

THE EXPECTATION OF DECLINE: FACT AND FICTION

For many people, the expectation of physical and mental decline becomes a self-fulfilling prophecy—expecting an event tends to cause it to happen. We are all fed a great deal of negative and often false information about what will happen to us as we grow older. As we have noted, the elderly are portrayed as more rigid, less able to learn, and more forgetful than younger people. In a recent study, a group of 25-year-olds, for example, believed that the effects of aging could be seen at 35 and that by 45 the person was "on his or her way over the hill."

For many people in our population, these stereotypes are taken as reality, so that each tiny ache or pain or lapse of memory that they experience is taken as a sure sign that they are getting old and consequently cannot perform as well as they had previously. As a result, their spirits flag, their self-image suffers, and they may cause the very effect they fear. They also often get reinforcing negative feedback from their contemporaries and love to return the favor.

While many older people are experiencing active, healthy, fully involved lives, with no hint of decline, such cases are often dismissed as exceptions, because "we know" that our abilities decline with age—despite the fact that there is no conclusive evidence that age causes changes in ability and behavior, although it may be a contributing factor in specific cases.

At certain occasions, it may not be a decrease in actual productivity but a resistance to change (an attitude that in itself can be changed), rather than a lack of ability, that creates the perception of decline. Most studies, however, have shown little difference in productivity between younger and older workers. To the contrary, a recent survey of copywriters age 45 and older demonstrated that older writers can still come up with fresh, creative conceptual ideas and successfully compete with much younger candidates, producing with more reliability for their organizations.[3]

The critical factors are the job that the person is doing as well as the traits and personality of the specific individual. Many conditions can affect the older worker's performance. For example, education, health, temperament, and upbringing are known to have a significant impact on people's intellectual performance. In this respect, the elderly are as different from each other as are members of any other group. Those who come from an affluent upbringing and, therefore, had less hardship in their lives tend to more easily maintain their level of intellectual competence. However, studies of the National Institute on Aging have shown persuasively that the majority of people are able not only to maintain their intellectual ability as they grow older but in some cases to improve it.

WHAT OLDER WORKERS CAN CONTRIBUTE

Many older people develop, on and off the job, skills in counseling, coaching, and communicating that can be useful for the organization for which they work. In the role of a mentor some people can be of great service to their younger peers. Mentoring is described as a developmental relationship where one person invests his or her know-how and effort in enhancing another person's growth in insight, perspective, knowledge, and skills.

The word "mentor" comes from Homer's epic work *The Odyssey*, in which Odysseus, while fighting the Trojan War, entrusts his close friend Mentor with the education of his son Telemachus. Mentoring can be an exceptional experience for both mentors and mentees, as their relationships may lead to successful changes and to memorable and inspiring results. We all remember our best teachers because they were able to reach beyond the curriculum and to touch our lives for the better.

Three particular characteristics help older workers to offer their help and views in greater depth and breadth.

- *Maturity.* A solid body of research indicates that older employees tend to make up their minds more slowly than younger ones but consider more factors when doing so. Their judgment tends to be sounder, though they are less inclined toward risk, particularly impulsive risk. This does not mean that older people are inherently more conservative than younger people. Taking advantage of one's lifelong experiences should not be confused with fear. Timidity, uncertainty, or a tendency to avoid hard decisions is most often a lifelong behavioral pattern that affects some people and not others. Mature behavior and judgment are a primary asset to any organization.
- *Synthesis.* Older workers have collected a lifetime of observations, facts, and data. At some point, often in the prime of their life, they

may begin to synthesize this learning in comprehensive ways. Older people begin to build elaborate and often elegant systems of thought that allow them to extrapolate and to draw new conclusions about their experience. These insights form the basis of a personal philosophy that can be of value to the organization. It is a rather special period when older managers can make a particular contribution toward influencing the directions that the organization under their leadership will take. The ability to synthesize is a natural result of processing experiences. It is, however, rarely recognized, and few have been taught in a systematic way to do this. Assigning certain challenges to older workers, sharing current information with them, and seeking their counsel can go a long way toward encouraging such distillation of experience and the advent of new approaches to solving certain problems.

- *Creativity.* It takes ideas to come up with ideas. A large part of creative thought emerges through the process of association, that is, seeing the similarity or dissimilarity between new ideas and the things we know. This often requires making the intuitive leap between what is and what could be. The more experiences we have stored in our mind, the more we are likely to see the connection between a need and a unique solution. Experience not only leads to more reasoned decisions but also imbues the individual with a greater sense of self-confidence. Having more flexibility in assignments and deadlines, older workers can pursue more creative solutions to company problems than their younger colleagues, who are often hampered by inexperience and anxiety. There is a different and quite beneficial aspect of creativity: to the older person, it provides a positive outlook, a sense of well-being, and opportunity for personal growth. In this way, creativity and experience come together as a unique inner resource for older workers' vigorous efforts and unrelenting energy.

KEEPING OLDER WORKERS PRODUCTIVE

Marc Freedman, author of the book *Prime Time* and of many articles on the issue of aging, feels that we are in the midst of creating a new phase of life between the middle years, when careers are winding down and children move out of the house, and true old age.[4] "While the old retirement ideal will continue to hold sway for some," he says, "many others are looking only for a temporary pause—to catch their breath after long years of midlife work—before tackling the next challenge." Freedman adds that this growing population of older Americans is the best educated we have ever known. "There has been an unprecedented societal investment in developing the skills— professional, managerial, and otherwise—of this population. The number of people who have attended college has quadrupled, and we've witnessed a proliferation of professional degrees compared to previous generations."

This reinforces our earlier observations that organizations will have to shed many of the customary and well-known misconceptions about older workers and respond differently to issues related to their aging workforce. Older workers don't want to be sidelined; they require continued investment in their professional abilities and are looking forward to a climate of responsive openness with their employers as a basis for job satisfaction and ongoing motivation.

Organizations are to keep older employees productive in essentially the same way younger employees are kept productive—by providing them achievable goals, by giving them due recognition for their accomplishments, by providing them meaningful work, by offering them opportunities to grow, and by making them fully functioning members of the work environment. Employers will be rewarded by older employees' work ethics, by their values, and by their sense of community, which will be imparted to the rest of their workforce.

There are a few particular recommendations, however, to support a broadly intergenerational work environment. Ron Zemke et al., in *Generations at Work*, call them the ACORN imperatives:[5]

- *A*ccommodate differences and consider employees' special needs.
- *C*reate workplace choices, allowing the environment to shape around people. A relaxed and informal workplace makes old and young more comfortable.
- *O*perate from a more sophisticated management concept, with managers relying on their "personal" power earned by people's acceptance, respect, and recognition. Management should focus on the big picture, on coordinating efforts and serving as a source of expertise

and at the same time turning people loose and allowing older workers to use their experience for counseling and mentoring.

- *Respect* competence and initiative and trust your people.
- *Nourish* retention by broadening assignments and offer new skill opportunities to both older and younger workers.

Zemke feels that successful intergenerational teams are helped by aggressive communications and what he calls "deliberate diversity." It is important to eliminate the dividing lines between young and old, interconnecting all partners of a work group.

In summary, we must be careful not to squander the resources of wisdom, experience, and talent that are older workers!

A few questions to consider:

- In your own organization, are the contributions and experience of older employees being valued? What are some of the attributes that make them valuable?
- Does the culture of your organization facilitate the inclusion of older employees in terms of their acceptance by younger colleagues and a general willingness to share ideas and information?
- Often we see the advantage offered by older individuals in three particular characteristics: maturity—the value of their experience; synthesis—drawing conclusions from their life-long learning; and creativity—creative thoughts based on the process of association. Have you been able to make similar observations in your own organization?

Senior Citizens Only — The World of
Vita Needle Company

"Wow—this is unique." That's what Larry Christian thought when he joined Vita Needle Company of Needham, Massachusetts, back in 2002 and noticed all the senior citizens working in production. He had moved here from Illinois and had a human resources background from his previous job. "You come here and see what's happening—it was almost stunning," he marveled.

Vita Needle Company is a fourth-generation family business, founded in 1932 during the depression years. The company manufactures reusable needles for veterinary applications and for all kinds of industrial purposes, along with tubing, adapters, and fabricated parts. Over the years, it has built a reputation for quality, good price, performance, and reliable service.

"The company hasn't always hired retired people," Larry explained. "In the 1930s and 1940s they recruited regular workers. But in the last ten to fifteen years they mostly hired senior citizens."

Vita Needle Company is located in the middle of town in an old dance hall and former theater built in the 1920s. One can still appreciate the old stage with wonderful carved woodwork as well as the box office around the corner in one of the hallways. The production is set up on the old dance floor, revealing the original oak boards. Production stations are organized in rows with different pieces of equipment for cutting and grinding the tubing, for staking the needles into hubs, and for burnishing and polishing.

The surprising aspect was to see all the white-haired ladies and gentlemen sitting in front of the machines. Vita Needle Company employs about 35 workers in production, 95% of them part-time senior citizens. "They are in a group of their peers," Larry pointed out. "Every one of the people out there has a responsible job. They have work to get done and they get it done."

We had a little roundtable conversation with three of the production workers—with Rosa Finnegan, 93 years old and with about 9 years at

Vita Needle Company, with Bill Ferson, age 86 and with more than 17 years with the company, and with Dick Tompkins, age 78, who joined the organization just 2 years ago.

Rosa Finnegan had worked as a waitress most of her life. "I retired at age 65," she said, "didn't enjoy it and went back to waitressing for a while." Rosa's husband had passed away, and her son with two grown-up grandchildren wasn't enough to keep her busy. "I was living alone," she continued, "and went to the Cape to live and didn't like it. When I came back here, I remembered about this place and that they hired older people. I asked for a job and they told me I could start tomorrow. I have been here ever since."

Rosa was trained by the shop manager. Was she afraid in the beginning, with all these machines? "No," she responded, "I was so anxious to find something to do that I just wanted to learn whatever they asked me to."

Bill Ferson was much better equipped for his job at Vita Needle Company. He had worked for almost 40 years for a manufacturer of measuring gauges and afterward joined his former boss in a new company, producing parts for gyroscopes. That venture lasted for another eight years until Bill decided to retire again.

"At my second retirement," he told us, "I was 69 years old. When I was out for a few months, I didn't like it. I was always active. Then I saw this little ad in the local paper, came down here, and they hired me. They wanted to put me to work right away, but I said: 'Wait a minute; my wife doesn't even know I am here.' She didn't know I was looking for a job. I left here, went home and told my wife: 'Guess what, I may go back to work tomorrow.' She said: 'Good. Gets you out of my hair.'" At that point, everyone around the table had a good laugh.

"I have been here for 17 years," Bill continued, "and I have no intention of giving up work. I think, at our age if you are able to work, it's better for you. It keeps you sharp. And I am very happy to be with people my age. We get along good, [even when] we fight once in a while." Across the table Rosa was chuckling.

Dick Tompkins was employed by the railroad for almost 14 years and went on to work for different freight airlines, like the Flying Tigers, for another 26 years. At that point, Dick could have retired, but he decided to stay on for another 14 years in a sales capacity with a freight forwarder.

"Then I decided to retire," Dick said, "but after a few months, I got tired of sitting around. I wanted something to do and I always knew about Vita Needle. Then, when I saw their interview on *60 Minutes* and their emphasis on senior citizens, I thought that's the place to go. I got interviewed and came to work here for almost two years now."

We asked how he felt about working on the production floor. "I don't work with machines," Dick explained. "When I came, they were shorthanded and needed somebody in packaging. I like it, it never stops, believe me. [In 2004] the company had a banner year, one of their best years. As we were discussing, they have a variety of products— some minute—they have to be counted and then packaged. You wouldn't believe the customer requests. Everyone wants it packaged differently, in a different set-up."

We questioned if the needles have some kind of standard packaging. "No, no," Dick went on, "it's variable, you wouldn't believe it. They [are packaged] six in a bag, loose, or packed on a card with cellophane around it. And then we put all types of different labels on them. Some don't want our label, to others it does not matter. There are lots of variables."

At that point, Bill Ferson chimed in: "I would like to put a little plug in for my coworker Rosa. At her 93 years of age, you would like to have six people her age working for you." We asked what he meant by "working for you." Was there a lot of structure? What about supervisors?

"There are Mike, Tim in production and Larry in customer service," Dick responded. "They [are available] for any questions we have." "They feed us the work," Bill added, "and we take it from there. We got them to fall back on."

But, when all of a sudden Mike, a younger guy, became their boss, how did they like that? "No problem," Bill said. "I went through the same experience. I worked myself up in my former company and then had 45 people under me. I had worked with Mike, before he became my boss. He had worked here part-time. I knew him; I knew his father before that and his grandparents before that. His father is my age, they owned the market."

We questioned if Bill ever had a problem with Mike and what he did about it. "Oh yeah," Bill reminisced, "we discussed it and talked it over. If we have some argument, we work it out. You do that no matter where you work." Rosa added: "If you can prove that you can do something better, different from what he tells you, he'll say: 'Well, let me see' and, usually, he'll go along with you. And no one says 'hurry up,' there is no pressure here."

Vita Needle Company always produced and sold reusable needles. Some years ago, the medical market changed over to disposable needles, and the company fell on hard times. They switched to a variety of new fields, getting into all kinds of specialized needles for industry and retail. They also started to manufacture and offer tubing and wires. Was it difficult to adapt to all these changes?

"No," was the unanimous response. Rosa added: "We all do different things and we all learn every step of the way. [Therefore] you really are not doing the same thing day in and day out. It's all very interesting because you are always learning something new."

As a matter of fact, Rosa, with her background as a waitress, got quite experienced in her new job and has been working all over the shop. "[In the beginning]," she explained, "I was anxious to find something to do so that I just did whatever they asked me to. [Today], there are so many different steps, doing 'hubs' and gauges, stamping the needles, drilling, then packaging—it's fascinating."

People at Vita Needle Company are pretty much able to set their own hours, and many of them have a key to the facilities. "Bill and I," Rosa continued, "and another gentleman are here at 5:30 in the morning. There isn't a boss here to tell us what to do, but we all seem to know what we have to do. It's wonderful to wake up and have somewhere to go."

How true this is! And there is a lot of camaraderie and concern for each other. Bill alluded to it: "We kind of watch out for each other. We have a little system here—if we don't show up, people are going to call and look after you." Rosa summed it up: "I think working here has been one of the things that keeps me going."

An amazing interview with inspired senior workers! "It's interesting to interact with people of the kind you saw," Larry told us later. "Their standards, work ethics, and everything like that are so much different from what they are with people who join the workplace today. You heard Bill say 'nobody is standing over us' and you don't have to."

However, how do you keep deadlines with customers when you are not always free in your schedules? "That's right," Larry responded, "our speed of working and the way we can handle things are figured into our lead times. People have their problems with ailments and you have to make allowance for that. [But] just because you hire senior citizens, it doesn't mean that you cannot compete in the marketplace. We advertise that 'we are the low-cost producer' and we can beat anybody's price in our niche market. And that's by working with our senior citizens, their work ethics and things like that." A strong and affirmative statement, which speaks to questions of work motivation, productivity, and creativity of older workers!

We talked once more about possible difficulties of having a younger supervisor in charge of this senior workforce. "The pros outweigh the cons," was Larry's opinion. "If you plan your business correctly, you'll come out ahead. As far as the people having a younger person as their boss, I don't think it makes a difference to any of the seniors out there. I cannot think of one of them, at this point in their life, who would want to take [supervisory] responsibility. They would rather be given a job, 'tell me how to do it, leave me alone and I'll get it done.' I don't think there is that kind of a conflict."

Vita Needle Company is a unique organization that has been widely recognized for its practice of integrating senior citizens into its workforce. Obviously, there are cost considerations—seniors are eligible for Medicare and have no need for company-paid health coverage. But, as owner Fred Hartman once said: "They don't have the PTA [Parent–Teacher Association] meetings or the kids in day care." He finds them loyal and responsible. To work is a high priority for them.

Vita Needle Company has been covered in the news media and also by several European TV stations that wanted to show their viewers, Look, this can be done. In that context, Bill told us, "We received a letter from a woman [of the TV team] over there—I forget her age— who had to retire. She said: 'I have to sit here on the sofa and die. [Instead] I would love to be over there and go to work for you people.'"

Which brings back the echo of Rosa's revealing remark: "It's wonderful to wake up and have somewhere to go."

CHAPTER 6

Successful Safety, Health, and Wellness Partnerships

Every organization and every employee therein has a responsibility and challenge to do what it takes to enhance employee safety, health, and overall wellness. This responsibility does not diminish as the workforce ages, nor does it necessarily become any more difficult. Unfortunately, in the realm of health and wellness negative myths and misconceptions about older workers and their value in the workforce all too often find fertile ground.

Not surprisingly, supervisors with their responsibility to ensure that the work gets done each day are much concerned about employee illness and absenteeism. Excessive sick leave, tardiness, time off for doctors' appointments, and low levels of output because the worker is "not feeling well," even though being present, all reduce productivity. Ill health in the supervisory and managerial ranks is also of great concern, for low levels of energy, absence, or on-the-job illness can adversely affect decision making, continuity of operations, or output. Since frequent and severe illnesses are often associated in people's minds with advanced age, the treatment of addressing the issues of safety, health, and wellness of older employees has long been influenced by the belief that older workers represent a far greater health risk than other personnel.

Yet considerable and growing evidence indicates that many of these attitudes and beliefs are not well founded. The health of the elderly is, and has been, changing rapidly for the better in recent decades. Most of us have known a sprightly octogenarian who still does his or her own housework, attends the family business daily, or works part-time in a store or office. Perhaps we have heard of someone "way past 65" who performs heavy work, walks long distances each day, or "hasn't missed a day of work in the last 50 years." Such people are often regarded as exceptional or remarkable. There is evidence, however, that in the decades ahead such people will become very commonplace, and, as we demonstrate later, the elderly compare quite favorably with young workers when it comes to sick leave, tardiness, and low performance because of "not feeling well."

An individual supervisor, the managerial team that runs an organization, and the policies and procedures under which all its workers operate can all have an effect on an employee's health, attendance, and productivity at any organizational level. In the sections that follow, we consider the special and genuine problems related to the health of all older workers (even volunteer workers).

WORK AS A CONTRIBUTION TO EMPLOYEE HEALTH

We have generally sensed that work is a healthy activity and that prolonged idleness can debilitate the body, mind, and spirit. While this viewpoint can certainly be carried to extremes, we know, deep down, that if humankind had no work to do, it would probably invent it out of boredom. This idea might be challenged by those who experience their work as only onerous, demeaning, or unrewarding, but think of how many people serve in voluntary organizations, take on difficult, demanding hobbies, and invest considerable time and effort to generate wealth far beyond what they will ever use. All this is work—the expenditure of time and energy for some useful and productive purpose.

When we get past the notion that work is something that we *have* to do in order to survive, we tend to acknowledge that work, usually through employment, offers a person a wide range of rewards that meet a variety of physiological and psychological needs. This ability to master our situation and to meet our own needs provides a healthy balance in our life, an opportunity to grow and develop, and often the physical and mental challenges that keep us alive and alert.

At an elementary level, employment offers the regularity or rhythm of activity that may be missing in a retiree's life. This regularity is important to people who have based their life on routine, but it is also of importance to many others as a way of keeping their physical and psychological systems in tune. Further, for many, work provides physical and mental exercise that keeps their body and mind from atrophying. For older people who lack adequate resources or income to play or work as desired, a job may mean the difference between want and adequate shelter, a healthy diet, and even survival.

For most, income-producing work means "freedom from fear"; it means meeting our body needs and the inherent need for security that is so strong in humankind. Regular work, however, is associated not only with income and financial security but also with the sense of calm that comes from knowing that there is something waiting for us to do, something that has value to others. How did Rosa Finnegan of the Vita Needle Company express it so well? "It's wonderful to wake up and have somewhere to go."

The awareness that a paycheck is given for value received is very explicit and concrete. This sense of worth and utility is clear for every day of employment, and this builds self-confidence, good inner feelings, and a secure belief that anything so necessary is not likely to be swept away.

Another important aspect of work that contributes to health is the inherent and genuine "stroking"—the interpersonal recognition that comes with possessing a job. The companionship, sense of acceptance, and feeling of belonging that friends at work bring to each other provide the mind-body link that can counteract forms of marasmus, or wasting away, that often comes to some who live isolated lives. The hunger for meeting these fundamental needs can help keep us healthy.

Thus, having a job maintains self-esteem and pride, that sense of distinction and accomplishment that virtually everyone needs. Though a job may be little valued by its holder until it is lost, even retirement is seen as something earned through work. Some types of work provide far more healthy recognition and challenge than others. Boring, dead-end, highly regimented work affords little in the way of health-generating good feelings, while highly exacting, intense, and unrewarding tasks can create debilitating stress and tension. Therefore, the kind of work and the way it is organized, paced, and supervised can have much to do with whether it contributes very much to the physical and mental well-being of the employee.

CAPACITY DEVALUATION

Older people disabled by accident or illness tend to be treated differently than are younger people with the same type of disability. Our society's orientation toward chronic conditions, impairments, and capacity losses all too often leads to barring many displaced or disabled workers from jobs. Many people mistakenly consider impairment as a disability, and this distortion leads us to regard impairment as the only real criterion of disability. This focus on medical impairment directs attention away from job performance requirements, an individual's adaptability, and the flexibility of job requirements and toward the more definable, but less adaptable, condition of impairment. Thus, if a person were to suffer a severe (say 50%) loss of hearing, the impairment would be seen as a disability, regardless of whether the impairment actually reduced the person's ability to do the job, whether the job could be modified to permit adequate performance, or whether the person was able to compensate for the impairment.

Older workers who believe that their capacities are devalued and that therefore it will be difficult for them to keep or find work tend to accept illness and incapacity as a socially acceptable way out. Such a person tends to turn into the kind of individual the situation requires—a disabled one. A recent study finds that "the acceptance of disability and the requirement of proof by regulatory agents are also consistent with increased commitment to behavior and attitudes appropriate to incapacity. The association of aging with capacity loss leads to the identification of chronological age as, in itself, a measure of capacity."[1]

"Sadly," the above study continues, "the evidence on older worker attitudes suggests that self-regarding attitudes are fixed early in the course of incapacity." However, it also notes that "we can successfully intervene in this self-devaluation of older people and minimize its effect, especially at the outset of incapacity . . . rather than as a restorative treatment after they accept their disability." Thus, the study makes a clear distinction between capacity loss and disability. It further states that "a substantial proportion of older men [and women] become severely disabled who might otherwise make a more productive adjustment to disability. Employment and rehabilitation practices, however, systematically limit [their] adjustment opportunities, and negative self-evaluations lead to inflexible and maladaptive responses." Health and work attitudes play a critical role in the success or failure of older people to continue to work regardless of the capacity loss involved or the extent of physical recovery.

In addition, studies in Britain found that "attitudes (emotional problems) of older working people were more important factors in hardcore absences from work for sickness than the original physical condition."

The amount of time off work for illness or injury also was found to affect productive reemployment. "It appears that if a person has three months off work at any time in later middle-age, there is a [substantial] risk they will never return to work again." This fact has led many researchers to suggest that, just as hospital patients generally recover faster if they get up and around soon after surgery, disabled or ill older employees should be allowed to return to work (or at least given something productive to do) as soon as it is medically feasible. The longer a person remains idle, the more likely idleness is to become a lifelong pattern that often leads to further decline and possibly to an earlier death.

Since these facts about health and wellness have been known since at least the late 1960s, why are organizations so slow to adopt policies that would improve the productive lives of many older employees? Part of the answer may be ignorance among policymakers, but much of it also seems related to our general tendency to accept the ill health of older employees as natural or inevitable and to expect them to retire or get along as best they can.

When President Carter signed ADEA legislation in the 1970s, many of the bill's strongest backers linked premature retirement with ill health to early death. Many physicians share this concern.

While physiological changes are most pronounced and most associated with age, they vary markedly among individuals of the same age. This suggests that we should focus on the health and wellness of each individual rather than on the age group to which an individual employee belongs.

THE DISABILITY ISSUE

According to the U.S. Social Security Administration, approximately half of the older workers who retired in the early 1970s did so because of disability. Yet as the U.S. economy has shifted from physically demanding jobs to those in the information and service industries, more people are able to work longer. The percentage of workers 65 and older in finance, insurance, real estate, and wholesale and retail trade already is today nearly four times the percentage of such workers in all other industries combined.

Governmental and private programs to improve health conditions in the workplace (such as asbestos removal) and prohibitions against the use of toxic and carcinogenic substances in manufacturing and processing industries have had a substantial, long-term, beneficial effect on the health of older employees. Similarly, while many workers over 65 suffer from chronic diseases such as declines in sensory processes (especially vision), degeneration of the immune system that can lead to kidney or cardiovascular diseases, and irreversible diseases such as rheumatoid arthritis, such conditions can often be controlled medically so as not to impede a person's ability to work. A successful cataract operation on an 80-year-old may restore that person's effective vision to its level at age 40.

Some older employees become trapped in a downward health spiral when hit by unemployment or the threat of it. The anxiety and stress of an anticipated layoff or job loss can demonstrably increase the likelihood of employee illness. If such a layoff actually occurs, it compounds the likelihood of psychologically induced sickness (which is a physical illness nevertheless). Since most employees' health insurance benefits are a function of their employment, loss of employment tends to lead to reduced health care. Consequently, such illness and reduced care may make reemployment even more difficult. This downward health spiral seems to be a major factor in forced employment withdrawal by many older employees.

Age provides a poor indicator of an individual's health. Some people's health declines rapidly with age, while others experience little or no decline for decades. In the general population, there is a tremendous variability in wellness among older people. Among the working elderly, there is even less correlation between age and ill health. When considering employee age and ill health, we should recognize that, first, unhealthy workers of any age tend to leave the workforce, so that those who remain are in better than average health; second, absenteeism and turnover, which are often associated with ill health, are less common among older than among younger employees; and, third, when poor health leads to poor performance, taking corrective measures that protect the interests of both parties is a major management responsibility and/or opportunity.

Some authorities claim that health is the overwhelming factor in the retirement decision. While surveys generally show that health is *stated* as the overwhelming factor, one source, discussing a Social Security retirement history study, suggested that the health factor may be exaggerated because "social pressures from a work oriented society may induce some older people to cite [health problems], rather than a desire for increased leisure."[2] The study found that of retirees who stated that they had no current health problems limiting the amount or kind of work they could do and that their health was *better* than that of their peers, over 10% nevertheless stated that health was their primary motive for retirement. Of those with no current health limitations who reported their health as the *same* as that of their peers, an average of 16% reported health as their primary reason for retirement. The study's conclusion is that "unless the health of all these people has improved since retirement, health status should not be accepted as the complete explanation for their early retirement decision."

Retiring "on" disability and retiring "because of" disability may be two quite different things. However, a kinder assumption is that even to those workers who retire on disability, health might be a way of resolving the psychological dilemma caused by the conflict induced by early life messages about "keeping one's nose to the grindstone," rather than a desire to escape from an onerous work situation or to enjoy more leisure.

INTELLECTUAL DECLINE

There has long been a popular notion, based on some rather faulty early research, that people hit their mental peak during their 20s and then begin a gradual, steady slide downhill until death or senility occurs. Such a belief can in itself needlessly damage people's health. For instance, when an older person becomes disoriented, begins to forget, repeats things frequently, or experiences a substantial personality change, many supervisors, coworkers, and even family and friends tend to regard such behavior as an inevitable part of old age. The older person may easily accept their assumption and consequently not seek medical attention for symptoms that in a much younger person would be considered serious signs of some sort of breakdown.

In reality, where intelligence tests have been administered to people as they grow older, researchers have found that most people maintain their intellectual ability through their 60s and often beyond. Some current evidence suggests that there may be some general decline between ages 70 and 80 as a result of normal aging but that it is usually not severe enough to impair a person's job performance. Even such decline may be lessened as more older people maintain their general health longer.

Many prominent researchers have concluded that any decline in intellectual ability, when disease is absent, is probably a result of apathy, boredom, and/or disuse of the mind. The only aspect of intellectual ability that appears to genuinely decline with age is speed of response. When rushed by others, older people tend to respond poorly. However, if there is evidence of rapid and noticeable mental decline, it is important to consider illness, not age, as a likely cause.

This leads us to the topic of senility. Many people believe that senility is inevitable in people beyond a certain age. In reality, less than 5% of our population will become senile, and some of this is increasingly reversible. Senility results from a brain illness or disease and is not a direct consequence of normal aging. We are all somewhat familiar with Alzheimer's disease, which is presently covered by an enormous amount of both private and government-funded research and seems to be close to at least a clearer understanding of the disease. At this point, there are some first therapy possibilities for Alzheimer's. Therefore, if an employee develops significant signs of "senility," it is important to encourage and recommend prompt medical diagnosis and attention. It is all too common for people in the workplace to express surprise at how quickly an older individual went downhill mentally (especially after an illness) without its occurring to anyone that the person may have had a treatable medical problem and with everyone tragically assuming that this deterioration is the inevitable consequence of age.

HEREDITY AND HEALTH

When we turn to physical health and vigor, we encounter a reality and a very common myth whose mistaken application can cause unfortunate consequences for the individual and the organization. The reality is that long, healthy life tends to run in families. The myth is that beyond a certain age (specified such as 55, 60, or 65, depending on whom you are talking to), it is expected that the physical health of many people goes steadily downhill, that chronic diseases increase dramatically, and that some people become bedridden for long periods of time, and, this is virtually certain.

Sadly, some people often use the reality that heredity affects one's longevity and health to reach some strange conclusions. For example, some people who know that early heart attacks run in their families often despair and wait fearfully for the inevitable to happen. Conversely, some people who are genetically well endowed (with four healthy, long-lived grandparents) perceive themselves as immortal and neglect the health measures that common sense should dictate.

Our genes are not the only things that affect our lives. Diet, exercise, family conditions, how we manage stress, and our social support system greatly influence how long and robustly we live. The fact that, *as of today*, men tend not to live as long as women and that people of a certain racial background tend to die earlier than others, and similar statistical data are sometimes used by personnel specialists and supervisors for questionable purposes.

What some people perceive as memory loss in some cases may be only a slowing of response time or inattention when information is first offered to us. However, with advanced age, usually age 70 or above, the normal loss of brain neurons, the circuits that control memory, may be significant enough that memory loss of 10% or more may occur, especially in our short-term memory.

Some people's brains are better at some things than at others. Some are good at formulating concepts or organizing information, while others may excel at storing details. Unless our memory loss interferes with our work or daily life, we should accept it as one of life's minor irritations and possibly look for other causes than age, such as stress, grief, fatigue, alcohol, or some other problem that can lessen our abilities in general.

Today, since genetics cannot yet be used for accurate predictions of individual health or longevity, it might be most practical to strive for a healthy lifestyle and expect the best.

SAFETY ISSUES

Since September 11, 2001, workplace issues, both individually and collectively, have taken on new dimensions. Also, as our economy shifts in the kinds of work people do, and as the environment in which they do it and the outcomes they obtain from it continue to change—with no end in sight—new safety issues arise.

A short look back can be helpful at this point. Generally in the past, the first-line supervisor knew more about a given workplace than any other member of management. Consequently, each supervisor had a particular responsibility for the safety and welfare of older workers and for ensuring that these workers avoided accidents. The wise ones sought the counsel and ideas of those workers to guarantee they were safe.

However, the increases in the numbers of older workers have strengthened this imperative. It has long been noted that occupational injuries occur at a lower rate among older workers compared to their younger peers. Work experience, particularly in industry, has demonstrated that occupational injuries steadily decline with age, up to workers age 65 and older. In other words, workplace experience could be a resource in designing some jobs and in employee training.

Yet, with some workers, their physical decline increased the risk of some hazards. For instance, falls on the floor and other work surfaces were more likely to result in bone fractures in older workers. Also, such injuries tended to be more severe and more costly to the organization. Five categories of injuries accounted for nearly 75% of all such cases, including sprains and strains; cuts and lacerations; contusions and bruises; bone fractures; and burns. As a matter of fact, fractures, hernias and heart attacks were significantly more common among older workers. However, with the general increase in "knowledge work" in our society many of these physical factors have declined in significance.

Nevertheless, older workers do get hurt, although most often accidents result from workplace hazards that affect all employees. However, it is not unknown that sometimes supervisors are also implicated by disabling certain safety devices to increase worker speed; by not adequately shoring up construction sites; or by setting delivery standards that prevent truck drivers from getting adequate rest—all to increase "efficiency." This is not only unconscionable but may tie up the organization's time and resources in lengthy and costly damage claims and lawsuits.

Consideration of those and similar factors in the case of older workers is just common sense and helps the supervisor to conserve his or her people resources. Also, safety training in general, relevant to each person's specific assignment, can provide significant benefits to employer and employee. In addition, the creation of a safety committee as a task force and everyone's attention to its findings can usually prevent most accidents. A common belief that "we work in a naturally safe environment" such as an office or classroom is often unrealistic. Slipping in front of a copier or stumbling on a tab of a carpet can cause as bad an injury as falling on the factory floor.

Coming back to the issue of terrorism, it must be mentioned here that it is hardly a new invention. It has been practiced since the earliest times and in virtually all societies, whenever people thought it might serve their needs and they could get away with it. There are many examples, but to discuss them here would go far beyond the confines of this chapter. However, terrorism requires a new shared responsibility between top management, supervisors, and employees. Everyone, old and young, needs to look beyond the walls of the organization and has to be attentive to sudden changes in the surrounding world. Everyone is called to show initiative, to be a watchdog, and to communicate closely with peers and management. Only a joint effort, based on mutual trust and cooperation, can help to prevent dreadful occurrences like the ones we have come to see in Oklahoma City and New York.

HEALTH VERSUS WORK

More and more older people are showing that the common belief that old age is a physical and mental toboggan slide is outdated. Today, many people are actually improving their health as they get older because of their increased attention to good nutrition, exercise programs, and the use of stress-management techniques. Many researchers firmly believe that while illness and decline can occur at any age, half or more of the decline experienced by older Americans is due to inactivity, boredom, and the belief that infirmity is inevitable. Active, involved, intellectually challenged employees with an effective social support system in the workplace need not necessarily experience a decline in their ability to get the job done.

The critical point is that, while most employees who are out of the labor force report health problems, a substantial proportion reports no chronic health problems or conditions that limit their ability to work. With this enormous healthy, but aged, resource idle, we may need to ask ourselves what can be done to encourage at least some of these people to become producers again. It is clear that many people work, produce well, and enjoy their jobs despite chronic physical problems. Perhaps some of management's concerns about the health and wellness issues in today's workplace are overdrawn. As our workforce ages, we may need to be more realistic and focus not on employee illnesses as such but on how they affect work output in individual cases.

STAY-WELL PROGRAMS

In recent years, a growing number of firms have developed employee health programs that concentrate on improving or at least maintaining employee health by encouraging healthy habits and preventive medicine. Such programs are often free to all employees, and in a number of companies the program is open to spouses as well. Employers gain much from promoting employee health and wellness, such as decreased absenteeism, reduced insurance costs, more consistent productivity, higher morale, and lower peripheral costs (such as hiring temporary personnel to fill in for ill employees). Employees can gain even more: greater ongoing health, feeling physically better more of the time, a prolonged life with fewer bouts of illness, and the good feelings that flow from self-mastery and personal achievement. Most of these programs are based on the following premises:

1. *Wellness* is our natural state and can be preserved through alertness, healthy habits, and early attention to developing illness or health problems.
2. *Lifestyle*—that is, the habits we engage in every day (smoking or not smoking, what we eat or drink, and so on)—have a major impact on the likelihood of illness and the length of our lives.
3. *Change* for the better of personal (and even family) habits can be achieved through positive encouragement and strong support from employer, coworkers, and supervisors.
4. *The workplace* is one of the most effective environments to encourage wellness, because so much of a person's time is spent there, because work requires a high energy level, and because the potential for transmission of disease from person to person is very high.
5. *Stress* as a primary precipitant of illness can be great or small at work, but it is there that the management of stress can be dealt with most effectively.
6. *Training* in how to manage one's stress, how to give up smoking, or how to properly engage in an exercise program can most effectively be offered by an employer.
7. *Support systems* such as medical examinations, employee assistance programs (drug or alcohol counseling), and the dietary offerings in

the employees' cafeteria are only a few of the ways by which companies and government agencies are able to encourage health and wellness among their employees.

At the core of stay-well programs is the paramount belief that each individual is ultimately responsible for his or her own health and wellness, and to an incredible degree each of us need not be passive or dependent on medical professionals for maintaining our health. Doctors may be needed to cure our illnesses or diseases once they have a hold on us, but proactive health habits can often be used to avoid that eventuality.

Wellness promotion in organizations has taken hold because of the observable gains derived by both employees and employers. One important source has stated that the reason for this increased interest . . . comes from four factors:

- The escalating costs of a sickness oriented health.
- The limited availability of health care professionals which, in turn, has resulted in an increased need to rely on self-help.
- The emergence of a more sophisticated [health care] consumer.
- A changing value system that places more emphasis on fitness, good appearance and moderation in many aspects of human behavior.[3]

Society in general and industry in particular are embracing the concept that "to stay well" is less costly than "to get well," that to *prevent* is more rational than to *cure*, and that a healthy lifestyle enhances the chances for improved health, longevity, and the quality of life.

While many major corporations have exemplary, comprehensive, long-term programs in health promotion, other organizations like companies, institutions, and government agencies offer stress-management training, promote employee sports teams, sponsor after-hours aerobics courses, and encourage employees to attend organizationally sponsored programs to fight alcohol and tobacco use, dietary problems, and drug abuse.

Nothing in a sound wellness program discourages employees from seeking medical attention when needed; such programs simply discourage passively waiting until illness takes hold before doing anything about it. The development of health-producing habits and a focus on illness prevention are becoming the first and second lines of defense in the struggle for wellness.

For older employees, this shift in orientation from a concern about illness to active efforts to generate health is critical. Unfortunately, older employees, especially less sophisticated individuals, tend to have lifelong conditioning to an illness-centered medical model of treatment. Further, certain poor health habits have been reinforced by decades of practice and social confirmation. Finally, many have been accustomed to deny symptoms, to avoid going to the doctor (males especially), and to disregard the advice they do receive. While these generalizations do not apply to the many individuals who are taking their health opportunities seriously, they do apply to a vast segment of today's older workforce. Therefore, the design of a wellness program can be critically important to older employees in particular.

DESIGNING A WELLNESS PROGRAM

Whether an organization offers a comprehensive stay-well program or can afford only limited assistance, several elements of a good design can have particularly beneficial effects on an older employee without a great investment in resources or facilities. Several of these elements are discussed below.

Developing Health Risk Profiles

Most health insurance companies have developed a process for identifying risk factors for all the major causes of death; the process, which is mostly computerized, can provide a comprehensive profile for each person at a modest cost. In many programs, participants have their blood pressure taken and a blood sample drawn and analyzed, as well as being weighed and measured. By filling out a questionnaire on one's lifestyle, mental outlook, and medical and family history, each person provides information that leads to a profile that not only identifies personal health risks but compares chronological age with "risk-age."

Perhaps most importantly, the profile shows how a person's "risk-age" can be reduced by changing certain behaviors. Most organizations follow up this type of profiling with programs and supportive systems that help people modify their behaviors for the better. It should be no surprise that the earlier an older person is profiled, the more profound the effects of the changes on that person's health will tend to be.

Managing Personal Stress

When a person learns to use a "relaxation response" (various meditative methods that produce a state of deep relaxation), to avoid excessive behaviors (such as eating too fast), to give up self-destructive habits, to cope effectively with external stressors that cannot be eliminated, to avoid being drawn into negative interpersonal transactions with others, and to take on healthy, satisfying behaviors (such as exercise or a productive hobby), that person's health usually improves dramatically.

Modern advertising would have us believe that headaches and upset stomachs are inevitable and that miracle pills will end the problem almost instantly. However, a headache or an upset stomach is a symptom, not a disease, and pill popping never gets to the source of the difficulty. Pills (unless prescribed by your physician for a specific ailment such as arthritis) should be kept as a *last* resort and used only as temporary relief while the source problem is being dealt with.

Every day, thousands of people are learning to effectively manage that great cause of illness—stress. When allied with proper medical treatment for existing specific ailments, stress-management techniques can lead to a healthier, happier life. Unfortunately, many older employees have been bypassed by such education and believe that discomfort and illness are inevitable "for one my age." Organizations offering stress-management programs can help these individuals particularly.

Democratization of Wellness Programs

A few decades ago, company health clubs were offered almost exclusively to executives. More recently, mid- and lower-level management as well as some professionals have been invited in. Yet, increasingly, organizations are realizing that they truly depend on *all* of their employees, not just on those they consider to be their elite. Nissan USA, for example, offers all its facilities and health programs to all its employees. But health and wellness programs do not necessarily require paying for expensive recreational facilities. Some of the wellness training and exercise programs can be delivered by outside agencies at their own facilities, such as the local school system, local recreation clubs, social agencies, or community colleges, at reasonable costs.

Developing a Comprehensive, Long-Term Program

A comprehensive, long-term program is not necessarily an expensive or involved one. It basically requires surveying employee needs or interests, identifying all of the components of a sound wellness program, designing the optimal sequence for providing them, and working out a delivery system that balances costs against anticipated results and organizational resources. An organization that has a company (or designated) doctor or nurse, for instance, can offer the services required for a health-risk profile inexpensively, and the results themselves may lead many employees to take remedial action on their own. Similarly, a smoking-cessation program offered through the auspices of the American Cancer Society a couple of times a year may be sufficient to meet one form of employee need. The organization's tuition-refund program may also be expanded to cover health-related learning outside the work environment.

Changing the Subculture and Developing Peer Support

Programs aiming at altering people's habitual behavior seem to work best when there are considerable peer support, an absence of negative messages from authority figures, organizational support, support at home, plenty of opportunity to practice the new behavior, and a network of similarly inclined people. Unfortunately, older employees may lack some of these supports, as, for instance, if they are widowed. But the most important consideration may be that planners of such lifestyle-change training ensure that the program has ongoing aspects that help participants stay with the new behavior. A person not only needs to learn what to do and how to do it but often needs help from people with similar problems to practice techniques and strategies for success. The new healthy behavior also needs to become "normative" for the subculture in which the person works. Here the supervisor can do much to encourage older employees to continue the new behavior and perhaps also run interference for those prone to accept negative peer pressure.

WE WILL PAY EITHER WAY

According to Miller, "in the United States the cost of health care for people sixty-five and over accounts for . . . one third of all spending for personal health care. Per capita the cost for the elderly is more than three times the cost for Americans *under* sixty-five."[4] Since germs are broadcast by everyone who is ill, how can we pass up opportunities to create a total healthy workforce and workplace throughout the organization? Preserving the health of older employees makes sense.

Overall, there is a great deal that virtually any employer can do to assist older employees to improve their health and wellness quotient. With constructive programs, policies, and support, they can help improve the lives of their employees in profound and long-term ways. But the most effective programs are those where the mode is one of partnership. Employees have at least as great a responsibility for their own health as anyone else has; working together, both employer and employee benefit.

How to Make Your Lifestyle Healthier

In closing this chapter, we would like to offer a few recommendations, taken from a workbook of one of the major health insurance companies, which may be of help in trying to change your behavior and making better life choices to improve overall health.

- *Eat a healthy, low-fat, and low-sodium diet.* A low-fat diet helps lower your cholesterol, and a low-sodium diet has a positive influence on your blood pressure. Both contribute to losing weight if you need to.
- *Choose healthy foods.* The American Heart Association recommends eating at least five servings (about one cup) of fruits and vegetables per day, limiting the intake of dairy products, meat, and egg yolks. As for bread and cereals, you should choose whole grain products whenever possible, as they contain soluble fiber, which also reduces cholesterol. High-calorie foods like sodas and candies should be avoided.
- *Check the food label for nutrition facts.* The label contains important information about fats, cholesterol, sodium, sugars, and, most importantly, total calories of food products. Your daily diet should not exceed 2,500 calories.
- *Get regular exercise.* With exercise you'll have more energy and sleep better. Walking is an excellent starting point—begin slowly and build up to at least 30 minutes five times a week.

Change involves learning new behaviors so as to form healthy new habits. Make change a priority, make it a commitment, and follow through. There is nothing wrong with asking for support. Friends and family may be quite ready and willing to help you.

CHAPTER 7

Training and Education

"You can't teach an old dog new tricks." Well, perhaps not, but since we are dealing with developable human beings and not "old dogs," the use of this commonplace saying is not only insulting but irrelevant. Most people go on learning virtually to the end of their days and adapt to life continuously. They may resist learning some things, as most of us do, and have no interest in learning others. But most older employees are quite interested in learning "new tricks" if they see a gain and if the required effort toward new mastery does not exceed what they are willing to invest.

Each older person, just like each person of any age, learns some things faster and better than others, has preferred learning methods, and finds different subject matters difficult or easy. Though certain factors make older people different from younger ones, when it comes to job training and education, these differences need not lead to a lack of success in learning.

There is another aspect to consider: the educational level of the older population has broadened considerably with the baby boomers coming of age. As of the year 2003, 90% of the workforce had finished high school, and about one-third had graduated from college. A higher level of education creates an incentive for continued learning and

leaves many of the common misconceptions about the intellectual
abilities of older people without basis.

MYTHS AND REALITIES OF TRAINING
OLDER WORKERS

Investing in the continued training and development of older employees is likely to be one of the most difficult and stubborn hurdles to
be overcome by the leadership of organizations, despite their growing
dependence on an older workforce. Discrimination against older
workers in offering opportunities for acquiring new skills and knowledge is well documented. Worse, denying such opportunities to people in their late 40s and beyond was, until a couple of decades ago,
openly and unassailably practiced on the rationale that investing in an
employee soon approaching retirement was "a waste" and certainly
not "good management practice."

Reserving training slots or educational opportunities for younger,
less seasoned employees was rationalized by other, often unconscious
biases. Younger people were considered inherently sharper, better
able to grasp the material, and less resistant to applying new methods or techniques. Along with these assumptions went the belief
that older people are set in their ways, experience declining intellectual abilities, have poor memories, and do not do well in classroom
settings.

The reality is that it makes more sense to keep training older workers because they stay with their jobs, while younger employees often
change jobs quickly. Of all age groups, job retention is highest among
the 55-to-64-year-olds, according to a recent survey of the Committee
of Economic Development.[1]

Another myth, that older workers are technophobes and unable to
make use of advanced information technology, is easily mitigated by
the observation, reported in the Media Audit, that between 1997 and
2000 people over 50 have been the fastest growing segment of Internet
users in the United States, reaching 38% of the total audience at the
end of the century.[2]

There is ample proof, however, that older workers are generally underrepresented in organizational training programs. As we see this happening, we have to realize that for older individuals the workplace setting often is the major source to continue their education and to update their skills. Continued and lifelong learning helps them to adapt to changing circumstances and to maintain much needed flexibility in their jobs. Yet many of today's older workers are casualties of the failure of business to provide future-focused training.

It's a myopic view of managers to reserve learning opportunities for younger people instead of offering them to the employee of 50 who may have 10, 15, or more years of service ahead of her or him over which to recoup the organization's investment. The challenge before us is to ensure that older employee learning is effective and returns a proper payback to the organization.

EFFECTIVE TRAINING OF OLDER WORKERS

Today, there is considerable evidence that older people, many still active at work, are interested in lifelong learning at quite an advanced age and make excellent students. As a good example, the overwhelming success of the Elderhostel programs shows the keen interest of older people in continued education. In similar ways, an American Association of Retired Persons (AARP) study, conducted in 1990, found that older students in college classes were as quick to learn as their younger peers. More than half of the older students interviewed stated that they attended campus events, read the student newspaper, and regularly used school facilities such as the student center and the library. They also mentioned that while learning provided the greatest benefit, they enjoyed the relationships on campus the most. The researchers also found out that most of the older students participated in many of the physical education classes. So much for the idea that older people, whether employed or not, are uninvolved in life and resistant to learning new things.

Harvey Sterns, professor of psychology at the University of Akron and chair of the university's program on industrial gerontological psychology, in a recent article summarized the scope of training programs directed toward older workers as follows:

> Effective training programs for older workers draw on principles used for effective training with any age group. The design of any training program should start with an analysis to determine where training is needed in the organization. The second step is a job analysis to identify what should be included in the training. The job analysis generates a job description that identifies the relevant tasks performed and the knowledge, skills and abilities necessary to perform the job. The third step is a "person analysis" to identify who should be trained. This may be carried out through performance appraisal and testing appropriate for the older worker.[3]

A number of important dimensions for effective training programs for older workers should be considered in their design:

1. *The structure of the training program should be carefully arranged.* A self-paced learning schedule allows older people to give the correct responses that are part of their repertoire and to perform better than they would with externally paced tasks. Self-paced learning methods tend to serve older learners well because they are noncompetitive and minimally stressful: the consequences of errors are not critical or threatening, since learners are able to practice the learning task until they get it right. In addition, the task sequence should be arranged in increasing complexity, "presenting easier aspects first. After mastery of the basic skills, more difficult aspects are introduced and practiced until the task or material is mastered. A reliance on task analysis appears to be a strong predictor of the success of the training program especially for complex tasks."[4]
2. *Materials should be relevant and realistically related to job needs.* It was found that older employees have a low tolerance for abstract and "nice-to-know" materials. "If possible, trainers should use former skills of the trainees and build on their past knowledge and abilities. Providing relevant . . . examples during training [or models that can be generalized] may also increase participants' attention, which would improve training effectiveness."[5]

3. *An older worker may need to be motivated to participate actively in training programs.* "Older workers' desire to learn may be impeded by fear of failure or feelings of inadequacy as compared with younger workers. Older workers who have had little formal schooling may have particularly low self-esteem. Motivation and self-concept can influence training involvement and success. Trainers can help alleviate feelings of fear or inadequacy by providing continuous positive feedback and reminders of training goals. Trainers should also ensure that managers and coworkers are giving support."[6]

4. *Participative teaching techniques that accent the learner's previous experience and accomplishments lead to high performance.* Learning methods that lead the learner through a series of positive learning experiences as a participating partner have much appeal for older workers, once they get used to the techniques. Many older employees have been raised in schools where the instruction was presented in a teacher–child mode, with the instructor imparting information top-down rather than sharing it as an equal. Also, like most of us, older learners respond best to encouragement, recognition, and a psychologically supportive environment. This is easiest to attain with active and participatory teaching methods. As a useful summary of these observations, "active participation is desirable for older trainees, because lecture or rote memorization formats may cause difficulty. Active participation may reduce cautiousness and hesitance among older trainees. Additionally, older workers' wealth of experience should enhance group discussion and learning."[7]

5. *Learning assignments requiring memorization often require more practice for older employees.* "Behavioral research consistently indicates slowing of reaction time and increases in learning time with age. Thus, slower presentation of training materials and provision of longer study and test periods should aid older workers. Given sufficient time, older learners perform as well as—or better than—younger learners. Self-paced learning is optimal. However, trainers should not just add more time without teaching efficient use of time."[8] There are different ways to compensate for memory problems to the extent that older people may perform better than anticipated. Most importantly, older employees can substantially improve their memory and therefore their performance through practice. Extensive

practice of a memory-based task soon lets an older worker match the performance of his or her younger colleague. Furthermore, research indicates that even a few practice sessions may be sufficient to produce a long-lasting effect on the memory performance of older personnel.

6. *Learning ability often declines through lack of practice.* "Training in learning strategies is a fairly new and rapidly developing area. The rationale behind such training is that we expect people to learn, but infrequently show them how to learn. [Older] adults may need training in learning strategies—either because they never developed them or they have forgotten them through lack of use. Examples of learning strategies include simple tasks such as rehearsal—for example, repeating the names of things to memorize. An example of a more complex strategy is outlining or creating categories."[9] Just as our muscles tend to atrophy from disuse, there seems to be a similar weakening of our mental capacity if it is not used. People should jog their minds as they do their bodies. Again, for the leadership of organizations, this highlights the issue of denying learning opportunities to employees who are advanced in age. Obviously, it leads to a self-fulfilling prophecy: for the older person it gets harder to be ready for training—and to do well if the chance does come along—which in turn leads the supervisor to conclude that more such efforts would be wasted. Instead, we need to seek out opportunities to keep an older person's learning ability alive. This includes challenging work assignments as well as the possibility to attend developmental programs.

7. *Testing and evaluation tend to be very stressful to older employees, and learning deteriorates rapidly as a consequence.* Though most people find testing stressful, older people seem to be particularly susceptible. This seems to be tied to self-image, a strong need to save face, and the fear of looking bad before younger peers. One of the rewards of aging is the respect and deference generated because of a person's age. To jeopardize that social standing can be very threatening. Closely related to that phenomenon is older people's tendency to avoid the risk of mistakes, which includes trying to guess the right answer. They may not respond at all to test questions for fear of being wrong and when the stress level is high. It is as though they are saying,

"doing nothing is not as bad as being wrong." In general, older employees do not like to be assessed against others and seem to learn best when measured against their own previous performance. This does not represent an aversion to meeting high job-related standards, but they simply like to do it their own way. To the contrary, an opportunity to show what they can do, in a job-related task, and given some time to master the challenge, is almost always well received.

OTHER DESIGN CONSIDERATIONS

Today, the challenge for trainers and teachers comes from a multi-generational and diverse environment, where each group—boomers, Generation Xers, men, women, and diverse ethnic groups—has unique perspectives and different preferences for acquiring, organizing, and applying information and skills.

In particular, in the older participants' group, where individual differences tend to be greater than among other age groups, it may be desirable and beneficial to provide more options in media and methods, greater flexibility in teaching approaches, and more attention to individual situations and needs. Some considerations to keep in mind are outlined below:

• *Generational differences often count in training and education.* The generation born before and during the Great Depression and World War II was the first benefiting from the notion that, at a minimum, a high school diploma constituted educational adequacy. The educational provisions of the GI Bill after the war, the growth of community colleges, and related developments in employee training raised national expectations to include a college education for virtually everyone determined to get one. Today, advanced degrees are the popular vision. Increasing technological complexity and work specialization caused similar progress in the training field. While baby boomers preferred an interactive and competitive learning style with opportunities for teamwork and networking, Generation Xers became frustrated with traditional schooling and insisted on self-directed, media-based, and multitask learning, which was supposed to be fun. Trainers were expected to be proficient and had to earn their respect. Successful training programs have to respond to those specific preferences, exploiting as much as possible the dynamics and tensions created by this multigenerational environment.

• *Cognitive styles.* Cognition—the mental process or facility through which knowledge is acquired, as through perception, reasoning, or intuition—is often related to the type and extent of education a person has received. Once acquired, a cognitive style tends to persist unless substantial efforts to change it are made. Therefore, cognitive styles are somewhat related to generational differences, with more structured and analytical styles in the older portion and a tendency to brainstorming and "lateral thinking" in the younger portion of our target population. Again, teaching methods should be adjusted to the strengths and abilities of each type of cognitive style, and supplementary assistance ought to be given where needed.

• *Gender, culture, and ethnic differences.* Some research indicates certain differences in the learning pattern of males and females within our own culture that result from the socialization process to which they were exposed as children and later in life. For instance, the macho self-image may produce less tolerance for potentially embarrassing situations and less sensitivity to the feelings of others in similar instances. Though many of these gender-related social differences are changing, it may take time until these changes reach the entire older workforce. As to some ethnic groups and people from other cultures, participants may expect and even demand a greater focus on lectures, rote learning, and even negative criticism. Again, individual attention to these participants and open discussion of training methods may be helpful here.

• *The key role of supervisors and managers.* Aside from formal training and education programs, supervisors and managers have a key role in challenging and mentoring people on their jobs. In today's organizational environment, managers are expected to become a source of experience and expertise, earning trust and respect as role models for the organization. In that capacity, in particular by coaching and mentoring, supervisors and managers are able to provide significant encouragement and support for the learning efforts of their older employees.

SUCCESSFUL TEACHING PRINCIPLES

The purpose of job-related training and education is not to do well in a test—it is to help successful job performance. Unfortunately, many people overlook this obvious consideration and structure their training in a way that turns off older learners, ignores their need for demonstrable results, and uses techniques that don't facilitate matters for them. The following are recommendations to make learning more effective for older workers:

- At the outset, provide an overview of the program explaining the needs and expectations of the organization
- Relieve learner anxiety before the program starts
- Plan for learning in easy steps of increasing complexity
- Introduce new subjects clearly and try to build on earlier knowledge
- Offer flexibility in teaching methods, showing individual participants how to absorb the material at issue
- Based on self-paced learning schedules, focus on the individual as much as possible
- Encourage participation instead of just imparting information top-down
- Use relevant and job-related materials and examples
- Consider all your efforts as a challenge to be met by you

Whether you are planning and conducting developmental activities for one individual or for a thousand, sound teaching principles can make all the difference with older learners.

DISCOVERY LEARNING

Validating the concept of learner-centered education and training, the "discovery learning" method attributed to Meredith Belbin seems to be one of the most productive approaches. It takes into account that older employees have a rich abundance of experience but often lack the ability to draw thoughtful conclusions and extract general principles from it.

The Discovery Method tries to help older workers to discover for themselves answers to a series of problem situations in a developmental order. Belbin's method consists of creating a sequence of specific meaningful tasks that require increasingly sophisticated solutions. Each task is relatively small and self-contained, having a meaning by itself. The instructor's role is primarily that of planning and creating the experiences and providing cues on approaches to solve a problem, as needed. He or she also may give quick feedback on mistakes so that incorrect learning is minimized. Participants have clear goals for each task, are allowed adequate time to practice, and have the opportunity to consolidate their learning before they go on to the next task.

The Discovery Method has been found to work well with virtually all adults, but particularly with older people because of its practical "apply now" approach. Discovery learning, with its strong emphasis on older learners discovering for themselves rather than having the instructor explain how to perform a task, has some valuable side benefits. The method helps train memory and fact retention, involves participants more actively in the learning process, and in the end significantly increases older workers' performance. It is particularly effective with people exposed to technology changes, to redesigned work, or to new responsibilities. Older employees, based on their rich experience, often develop highly creative methods to find solutions to the problems, which gives them a new sense of ownership and a strong commitment to their new work situation.

TO SUMMARIZE . . .

"Education and training provide important opportunities to facilitate career development at all periods in the working life of adults. Integrating work and learning is essential for continued adaptation in the work setting." These observations by Professor Harvey L. Sterns have much greater significance for older workers, who, at their stage in life and career, very much depend on continued challenge, growth, and achievement. For them, the workplace and related training programs often represent the major source of continued learning. The investment in training older employees—based on effective methods and sound principles—is an important and worthwhile proposition for future-oriented organizations. This is, in part, dictated by the demographic imperatives and helps to ensure the availability of experienced and talented personnel in a more competitive workforce environment.

What did we learn in this chapter?

- Today's "older workers" are much better educated than the generations before them. As the success of the Elderhostel program shows, older people are keenly interested in continued education and in lifelong learning. It helps them to adapt to changing circumstances and to stay flexible in work and life.

- Training programs for older employees are more effective if they are self-paced, allowing for ample study time and active participation. Learning strategies should consider older people's knowledge and abilities, avoid stressful tests and evaluations, and try to build motivation with support and positive feedback.

- Successful teaching principles include an initial overview of the program and the expectations for it, provide materials in easy steps of increasing complexity, and adapt learning schedules to individual capabilities. The method of "discovery learning" is particularly meaningful for older people as it allows them to find solutions to the posed problems based on their own unique techniques and to move on to the next challenge of increasing sophistication.

New Ideas from AES Corporation—
Older Workers as Pillars of a
Learning Organization

AES Corporation—a global power company headquartered in Arlington, Virginia—has a unique corporate culture, which we described in our earlier book, *New Corporate Cultures That Motivate*. A few years ago, AES went through some hard times as a result of the jitters of the ENRON scandal and overall restrictions within financial markets. Under the leadership of a new chairman and a new CEO, AES restructured its business, significantly lowered its debt burden, reduced its exposure in certain markets, cut costs, and generated substantial savings by centralizing certain functions. As of today, the company completed its restructuring and is back on its way to renewed growth and expansion. We closed our postscript on AES in the earlier publication with a comment by senior vice president Ken Woodcock: "It will be fun to look at us a few years from now." Well, it is indeed!

In an informative visit with Jay Kloosterboer, chief human resources officer of AES, we questioned if and to what degree the company's culture had changed and how AES looked at older workers as part of that culture. "Our fundamental philosophy, that those closest to an issue and with the most information are in the best position to make decisions, has not changed," Jay told us. "However, the reaction to recent corporate scandals established new requirements for corporate governance and has forced us to establish parameters and boundaries for what people can and cannot do. As a consequence, certain policies had to be modified. In today's world more people look over your shoulder, which isn't a bad thing."

"Sarbanes-Oxley and other similar regulations mean a lot more record keeping," Jay continued, "making sure that you have the proper documentation and the right level of approvals. It changed how we operate and took some decisions away from individuals who weren't in the best position to make those kinds of judgments. It pulled those decisions up to a higher level, with additional review."

Jay had joined AES about 18 months ago as part of the increased focus, mentioned before, on centralizing certain functions and institutionalizing certain processes. We asked him what the new human resources function was expected to accomplish. Jay felt he had two basic mandates.

"First, if you are really going to be a global organization that empowers people, as we strive to be, then you have to make sure that you have the best people in the right jobs. That was easy to do when AES was small. The people that started the company knew everybody and were able to judge which person was right for a particular job. But as we grew and acquired more generation, integrated utilities and distribution businesses, the ability to know everyone disappeared. Yet the fundamental belief that you needed the best people in the right jobs didn't change. So when I came here, I was asked to formalize and institutionalize a people review process that would work well as we continue to grow. A continued key to the success of AES is to have the right people in the right jobs."

"The other mandate," Jay continued, "is to transform AES into a learning organization—how to use the corporate group to share best practices and teach people around the [worldwide] organization. We work by taking what we do well in one part of the globe and transfer that knowledge to another part. And as we become a learning organization, one of the things we need to take advantage of is the knowledge that our older workers acquired over the years, and make sure it is being passed on."

Learning about different cultures and foreign customs is of particular importance to a global organization like AES. The best way to learn about doing business globally is to personally experience it. "Look at our CEO Paul Hanrahan," Jay pointed out. "He was encouraged to go to China and to lead our South American businesses. He was ready for the top job when it became available, because he was encouraged to have a broad array of challenging experiences. It wasn't by chance. We follow the same mantra encouraging people [to take new assignments], for both their personal learning and for their careers."

In earlier days, AES used to employ older and more experienced workers as "ambassadors" to help local people of new or recently acquired facilities to get going and to teach them the unique culture of the organization. Was this program still active?

"We don't use ambassadors any more," Jay responded. "As the program evolved, a few people got too focused on promoting the values, and not focused enough on the business. This undermined what was initially a very good idea. Today, we use experienced people from all over AES in new or acquired facilities to share our collective knowledge on a broad array of business issues, with our values and culture being a part of it."

We talked about the aging of the American workforce and about the fact that by 2012 almost half of the workforce will be between 48 and 66 years old. Baby boomers will by then be the "older" generation. "I have seen this phenomenon lately as I recruited," Jay confirmed. "But it is not a concern to us, we value experience."

"However, for us it's a little different," Jay went on; "90% of our employees are located outside of the United States." Indeed, AES Corporation's primary area of operation is not even in the older societies of Western Europe or Japan but in growing economies. "It's true," Jay told us, "the workforce in many of the countries, in which we operate, tends to be younger, with improving educational levels. It's different from Western Europe and other countries where social policy often encourages people to retire early. I don't understand how they can afford the social cost and loss of knowledge associated with those experienced workers."

One of AES' outstanding leaders in their global organization was the late Dave McMillan, recognized throughout the company for his accomplishments. Unfortunately, Dave passed away shortly after his retirement, and, to honor his memory and his legacy, the AES leadership established the "Dave McMillan Award for Leadership."

"It's a good example how we look at this," Jay explained. "The award is set up for special people, for a leader in the organization. You win the award by being that great business person, as measured by how you develop people. Individuals who develop other people possess a unique competency that we celebrate. They are people that may or may not be on a particular career track, but are great contributors to the company because they develop other people."

The yearly recipient of the award is described as "an extraordinary leader . . . who leads others to achieve things they may not have thought possible, and a strong mentor whose teams consistently achieve exceptional performance." In other words, this is the perfect challenge for the older individual who has the experience, knowledge, and people skills to achieve this and lead others to new horizons. Older workers as pillars of a learning organization!

CHAPTER 8

Building Motivation and Morale

What inspires people to work hard? What energizes workers to perform at high levels of effort and productivity? What make us strive persistently toward specific goals? For the last 50 years, these questions have been exhaustively analyzed by motivational researchers. The final result is that, in a very real sense, all motivation is self-motivation. We call it "intrinsic" motivation—a need that emerges from within us.

Let's take a moment to look at the understanding of motivation as it has evolved since the middle of the last century, to provide us with insight into the reasons certain organizations have been successful in generating high worker involvement and productivity. This is meaningful to the attitude of older employees, as they tend to be particularly sensitive to motivational issues.

EARLIER APPROACHES TO MOTIVATION

The important motivational theories of the 1950s and 1960s focused on human needs. These needs were seen as a motivational force, in that people would adopt particular behaviors to satisfy specific needs.

Based on this understanding, organizations developed sophisticated programs to appeal to people's needs for achievement and power, for self-esteem, and for social bonds. Managers were trained in how to evaluate, handle, and "motivate" their subordinates. Indeed, "motivational talent"—to be able to get others to work harder—became a desirable quality for upcoming managers. Looking at it another way, motivation was turned into manipulation.

This approach to motivation was strongly influenced by the work of Abraham H. Maslow and Frederick Herzberg. Exhibits 8.1 and 8.2 provide a more detailed account of their theories, along with citations on their most influential publications.

While Maslow's "Hierarchy of Needs" may not appear to be directly applicable to business settings, his ideas on people orientation, with their focus on human values and the need for meaning and purpose for one's work life, have not lost their impact. As to the needs in Maslow's "hierarchy," it must be remembered that all of them have an external focus. Even self-actualization had a Faustian quality of an ever-present, external driving force toward human perfection. Maslow conceived it as a "need." As we see further on, this is different from the joy and satisfaction of intrinsic motivation as we understand it today.

Herzberg's research, which expanded Maslow's ideas on the meaning of work life, proved to be more practical in its concepts and universal applicability. Its shortcomings can be found in the difficulty of an objective evaluation of the research findings as well as in the somewhat arbitrary differentiation between "satisfiers" and "dissatisfiers" describing the conditions of the work environment. Nevertheless, Herzberg's work had considerable influence and, in certain ways, had the current interest in the concept of empowerment following in its footsteps.

In summary, approaches based on need motivation have gained wide acceptance. Although this research has considerable merit, it doesn't get to the heart of the matter—the deeper emotional and mental phenomena that drive outstanding achievements in both our personal lives and our work lives.

EXHIBIT 8.1: **Abraham Maslow's "Hierarchy of Needs"**

Maslow's book, *Motivation and Personality* (New York: Harper & Row, 1954), and the concept of a "humanistic psychology" that he created must both be seen in their historic context. Maslow proposed a comprehensive life philosophy to counter Sigmund Freud's psychoanalysis as well as the behaviorist school of psychology, with its stimulus-and-response approach to motivating others. Maslow believed in the potential of humans to exercise choice, to grow, and to arrive at a point of self-actualization. Creativity, responsibility, and self-actualization were concepts of no consequence to either behaviorism or psychoanalysis. Maslow considered this a significant shortcoming.

The central piece of Maslow's theory is a pyramid of needs:

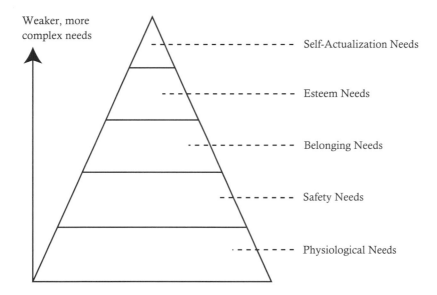

Maslow established the principle that needs generally must be fulfilled in sequence, starting from the physiological needs. According to his "prepotency principle," satisfying a lower-order need would enable a person to focus on the next higher need. Maslow's main focus, however, was on self-actualization. The drive for self-actualization might well advance even if there were a deficiency in a lower-order need.

EXHIBIT 8.2: **Frederick Herzberg's "Two-Factor" Theory**

Central to Herzberg's work is the so-called "two-factor theory," based on research on the job attitudes of 200 middle managers, mostly engineers and accountants. The study identified "job satisfiers" (later called "motivators"), defined as positive experiences that heighten job motivation. In addition, Herzberg listed "job dissatisfiers" (or "hygiene factors"), which were environmental and situational conditions that might lower job motivations if not properly structured.

The research asked people to think back to an experience that made them feel very good about what happened and then, alternatively, to recall experiences that made them feel bad. Analysis of these experiences led to the two categories mentioned above. The hygiene factors (dissatisfaction elements) do not add to motivation even if removed.

The most important factors in each category were as follows:

Motivators	Hygiene Factors
Achievement	Working conditions
Recognition	Supervision
Work itself	Interpersonal relations
Responsibility	Pay
Advancement	Policies and administration

In its conclusion, the study recommended increasing both job content and job responsibility by letting people run and improve their operations. Herzberg also advocated allowing for personal growth and self-fulfillment.

For more information, see Herzberg, Mausner, and Snyderman's *The Motivation to Work* [New York: Wiley, 1959].

THE CHANGING CONCEPTS OF MOTIVATION

Many of our earlier comments have focused on the difference between extrinsic and intrinsic motivation. Extrinsic motivation arises when people feel driven by an outside factor, such as a promised reward. In contrast, intrinsic motivation comes about by a strong emotional interest in an activity and by a sense of freedom and autonomy related to it.

Exhibit 8.3 lists sources of motivation and illustrates how the concepts of motivation have changed. The motivational factors above the diagonal line, which guided the earlier understanding of motivation, tend to be influenced by outside sources. For that reason, they lead to extrinsic motivation. In contrast, the factors below the diagonal line illustrate the findings of more recent motivational research. These factors come

EXHIBIT 8.3: **Our Changing Concepts of Motivation**

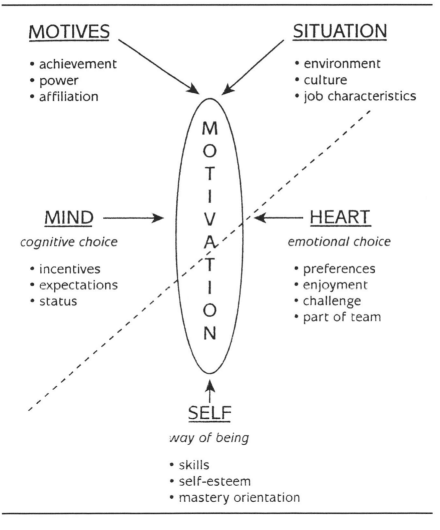

MOTIVES
- achievement
- power
- affiliation

SITUATION
- environment
- culture
- job characteristics

MIND
cognitive choice
- incentives
- expectations
- status

HEART
emotional choice
- preferences
- enjoyment
- challenge
- part of team

MOTIVATION

SELF
way of being
- skills
- self-esteem
- mastery orientation

from the inside, based on emotional choice or on an individual's self-perception. Therefore, the resulting motivation is intrinsic.

As we understand it today, intrinsic motivation is a much more powerful and lasting determinant of behavior than extrinsic motivation. Being in control of, and totally identified with, an activity is intrinsically motivating. Having the right expertise to meet an important challenge, being able to grow and to master new skills, and following one's goal of self-enhancement are all important drivers and sources of intrinsic motivation, and the opportunity to work as part of a close-knit team provides even further stimulation.

TRANSLATING MOTIVATION INTO PRODUCTIVE ENERGY

Summarizing our observations, there seem to be three major elements fostering strong intrinsic motivation:

- *Control and autonomy.* Motivation is at its highest level when people have full responsibility over their job. This means that they must be able to make major job-related decisions, to change procedures and make improvements, to innovate and be creative. In short, people who are in control tend to enjoy and fully identify with their jobs, which makes it a rewarding and productive experience. However, to let this kind of motivation occur, the role of management, as we have traditionally known it, has to change. Managers must learn to renounce the authority of their "office" and become a source of experience and expertise, supporting and mentoring their coworkers and earning trust and respect as role models for the organization. It's a difficult role; managers must avoid interfering in day-to-day activities in order to let people enjoy their freedom and autonomy.

- *Learning and personal mastery.* In several ways and in particular for older workers, learning is a healthy motivational experience. First, the very process of learning is highly satisfying in itself. In our lives, each of us has had to cope with a situation in which our skills were barely sufficient to handle a particular problem. Yet we managed to stay on top—an exhilarating and deeply motivating experience. Thus, personal growth translates into the ability to meet ever more difficult challenges. Second, learning refreshes us mentally, which is so important for the older worker. It keeps us flexible and helps us to adjust to changes in our business and in the economic climate around us. Creating this "learning disposition" adds to our personal mastery and self-esteem. Third, positive learning experiences help us to understand the broader context of our business and the interrelationship of its operations. We see our role in relation to our coworkers, which helps to respect their efforts and to build mutual support, increasing the group's productivity.

- *Work teams.* Teams provide motivational stimulus in different ways. First, work teams become kind of a "social anchor" to the individual. It is enjoyable to work with friends and to receive their support and recognition. But it goes further: group dynamics impact individual behavior and foster a certain role differentiation. Team members are allowed to choose their level of challenge: some become leaders, other followers. Or someone may be a leader at one time and a follower at another, depending on expertise, inclination, and situation. More important, however, this organizational structure makes it possible to assign responsibility for a meaningful work segment, even an entire work area, to a team. These broader and more important responsibilities create a different and more meaningful experience for everyone. Cross-training and flexibility within the team make the work more diverse and enjoyable.

Truly, you cannot motivate anyone except yourself. Management may provide incentives or disincentives—rewards or punishments—to an employee, but it is the employee who chooses whether or not to be motivated. We commonly speak of "motivating another person," but in a pure sense, people choose their own behavioral responses, though they may do so subconsciously and therefore "feel compelled" to react in a certain way. As an example, a company's culture may give rise to strong motivation of the people working there.

HOW HIGH MOTIVATION LEADS
TO GOOD MORALE

An obvious factor but one that is often overlooked is that motivation can as often be negative as positive. Managers who say, "I want motivated people" assume positive motivation from their perspective. However, often they have highly motivated people who are busy withholding commitment, diverting their efforts into personal pursuits, and spending their job time in social interaction with coworkers. This behavior implies a lack of motivation and is often based on discouragement and despair, so that neither the employee nor the organization benefits.

There is a small, but significant, difference between motivation and morale. Motivation tends to be goal-oriented, a drive to action, whereas morale is a more generalized phenomenon related to the condition of a person's involvement with, or commitment to, the organization. Thus, when people are demotivated, their goal may be nothing except filling a job slot and getting a paycheck. When a person's morale is low, the energy and focus needed to do the job are weak or absent.

As we mentioned before, an organization's culture has a significant impact on the motivation and morale of the people working there. A new kind of human relationship is the essence of healthy and motivating cultures. People have their ideals. They look for meaning in their lives, with work playing an important role in it. Instead of being treated as mindless laborers, people expect to be considered mature and responsible adults, capable of thinking, being creative, and being trusted. In these organizations, you see an unusual degree of interaction and communication, of a family or team spirit that helps generate motivational energy. People truly care for each other and share the joy of challenge and success.

MOTIVATING OLDER WORKERS

While it is difficult for anyone to reach high levels of work motivation, it is the more so with older workers, who are subject to so many misconceptions—"over the hill," "not adaptable," "out of touch with

technology," and many more. There are, however, two powerful motivators that apply to older workers in particular:

- Most older workers want to stay active and involved. They enjoy
  the mental and psychological stimulation of their workplace and
  are willing to commit significant energy to their job.
- Older workers appreciate the support and camaraderie of a close-
  knit work group where they are valued by their team colleagues for
  their expertise and experience.

Once older workers realize that they are being trusted and valued
for their work attitude, dedication, and expertise, they are ready to re-
ciprocate with a degree of commitment, loyalty, and productive effort
matched by only few of their younger colleagues. The older worker
draws his or her power from life experience, mature judgment, and a
sense of mastery, as well as from the habit of being responsible, the enjoyment of being part of a team, and the expectation of a positive self-
image. It's a potential of motivation and productivity waiting to be
unleashed.

THE MOTIVATION PARADOX

Curiously, many managers pay lip service to the values of morale and
motivation and then ignore them when making personnel decisions
about older workers. It is obvious that many organizations do not consider morale and motivation as drivers of productivity; if they did, they
would act differently. Unfortunately, the gap between management attitudes and official policies often is a wide one. It is doubtful that the leg-
islative changes eliminating age as a factor in mandatory retirement
have altered the difference between what managers of certain companies
say about older employees and how they discriminate against them
behind their backs. What is needed is greater congruence between words
and actions. Fortunately, there are quite a number of excellent firms—
Johnson & Johnson, Travelers Insurance, General Electric, Avaya,
Monsanto, and PepsiCo, among others—where, traditionally, official
policies have been matched by their appreciation of older employees.

COMMON SOURCES OF DEMOTIVATION

There is a variety of ways, based on bias or misconceptions, how organizations and their managers and supervisors undermine older workers' motivation. Often, such ways are unintended and a mere lack of sensitivity toward older workers' feelings. Other times, the old problems just don't seem to go away. Let's focus here on three major areas.

Age Bias

Discrimination of older workers, favoring younger folks for promotions and challenging assignments, still seems very much prevalent in today's business environment. Older workers are perceived as not having enough technological competence, not easily adapting to changes, and being hesitant to take risks and to make decisions.

We owe many of these misconceptions to the generation of baby boomers, many of whom were forever young, self-centered, and ready to move the older generation into retirement. While certain of the reservations toward older workers may be understandable, any deficiency can easily be mended with proper support and training. Much to the point, former labor secretary Alexis Herman stated at one occasion that "older workers are a resource that America cannot afford to squander."

Organizational Discouragement

Professional observers of older employees' behavior have often seen a "negative spiral" when an older worker receives a low evaluation rating, is left on a dull assignment for too long, or is passed over for promotion. Although this employee may initially put out greater effort, after not seeing prompt results, he or she may develop a "what-the-heck" attitude.

Similarly, managers and supervisors are often concerned that younger and promising employees, if dissatisfied, may move to another company and often to a higher level of compensation and responsibility.

Therefore, substantial salary increases, new and exciting projects, and promotions are used to hold on to these younger personnel. Older workers, on the other hand, are taken for granted and passed over when the goodies are passed out, in part because they feel locked in by their pension benefits and therefore may lack job mobility.

In addition, management often sees the need for greater human resource flexibility in case of a business downturn and subsequent downsizing. Older workers are perceived as immobile and expensive to let go, leading to strange reservations about keeping them too long or even promoting them.

The Curse of Obsolescence

Personal obsolescence often reflects inadequacies in the work environment that contribute to the insufficient use or the misuse of human talent. People lose their proficiency at a skill they are too infrequently called upon to apply. In addition, it is not uncommon for a supervisor (especially one with an age bias) to assume, without much detailed evaluation, that a deficiency in one skill characterizes the whole person.

When older employees see no chance for advancement or for challenging assignments, they may respond by just putting in enough effort to keep their job. There is little evidence that older workers are not interested in advancement or in a particular challenge, but they may withdraw from active involvement, become dispirited, and lose energy if they believe that their aspirations are being smothered.

Again, in a repressive organizational atmosphere, people may be motivated only by survival and security needs, not taking any risk and doing just enough to hold on until retirement. In this case, quite logically an older professional will not invest time in learning new skills, because the expectation to use them on the job is just not there. Instead of approaching their greatest period of creativity as they reach advanced age, older workers see their abilities atrophy, and they appear unable and unwilling to generate answers to the problems at hand.

In summary, in older workers it is important to stimulate their motivation along with expanding their abilities.

STIMULATING MOTIVATION AND MORALE

There are a number of ways by which managers and supervisors can help older workers to maintain and increase their levels of motivation and morale.

The Need to Learn

In his book *Age Power*, the author and psychologist Ken Dychtwald talks about the need to redefine our perception of "success" in the business environment. Instead of the earlier emphasis on status, power, and influence, we should begin focusing on achieving inner satisfaction, self-esteem, and personal freedom.

Adding to this thought, Gene Cohen in his book *The Creative Age* pinpoints the need for creativity. For older people, maintaining creativity provides a positive outlook on life and work and gives a sense of well-being. In advancing age, explains Cohen, the "unique combination of creativity and life experience" offers many possibilities for personal growth.

Older workers, indeed, are in need of opportunities to master new skills. Learning is a way of adding to their professional flexibility and helping them to more easily adapt to changes. Successful learning in itself becomes a source of motivation and builds self-esteem. It helps older workers to take on new challenges, to be ready for broader assignments, and to find inner satisfaction and a new purpose in their work life.

Organizational Encouragement

Many organizations have already instituted policies to help older workers to more easily balance their responsibilities of work and private life. As an example, the auditing company PriceWaterhouse-Cooper offers the option of a three- or four-day workweek to older employees, in order to allow for a less stressful environment.

Other possibilities are part-time assignments, the option of a phased retirement, or occasional sabbaticals to allow for study and technological update. Sabbatical leaves, which would allow full-time study every five or ten years, may not be too high a price to pay to keep a high-tech workforce at top performance. Full-time study of lesser duration may be an option, especially for new skills that are hard to learn on a part-time basis. Older employees often do best on self-paced, full-time study. Sabbaticals or full-time study can be seen as both a reward and an incentive.

Most importantly, however, organizations should clearly and forcefully prevent discrimination of older workers, defining a management philosophy as well as instituting rules and procedures that assure respect for their competence and trust in their loyalty and work ethics. This will go a long way in creating unusual work motivation and productivity in the older workforce.

Good Teams Get Better

Older workers are most comfortable in a work team that gives them a firm base of support and allows them to find their right level of challenge. The work team often becomes for them a "social anchor" as well. Being older, it is enjoyable for them to be part of a multigenerational team and to be recognized for their specific expertise and for their wealth of experience. Within such a work team, people may become leaders at one time and followers at another, depending on subject matter and situation. This helps to establish positive relationships of mutual support among its members.

We never quite understood the attractiveness of age-segregated living, as practiced in the "Sun Cities" of America. In view of what we said before, it would seem that older people are better served by eliminating divisive lines between the generations, interconnecting old and young through common values, and establishing a general sense of community.

Teams have enormous potential for enhancing motivation, as research by Harvard University professor Richard Hackman has proven. His studies suggest that team success leads to integration and togetherness. Being part of a successful team is stimulating and motivating to its members. Therefore, "good teams get better," which is particularly true for their older members.

WHAT DID WE LEARN?

In summary, there are several important steps to be considered to stimulate motivation and morale of older workers:

- We have to eliminate past practices and wrongful procedures, which discourage older workers and hurt their sensitivities, like age bias, organizational hurdles to challenging work and advancement, and preventing personal obsolescence.
- To stimulate motivation and morale of older workers, we first focus on their creativity and skill acquisition, offering opportunities for personal growth and professional challenge, leading to a renewed purpose in life and to personal well-being.
- Second, we need to put in place clear and forceful policies to support older workers and thus provide recognition and respect for their expertise and experience.
- Third, we best enhance older workers' motivation and morale by placing them into multigenerational teams, providing them with a strong base of support and a "social anchor."

We mentioned already an example for making good use of the unique qualifications of older workers. AES Corporation used to send experienced, longtime employees as "culture ambassadors" to new plants or recent acquisitions. It was their task to spread and explain the corporation's culture and the motivational spirit of the global AES team to new workers of "greenfield operations" or to the personnel of newly acquired facilities. While the company, for other reasons, has discontinued this practice, it still feels the need to take advantage of the knowledge of older workers, making sure it is being passed on.

These and similar ideas enhance older employees' morale and motivation considerably. In addition, an intracompany task force or a group of managers and supervisors may generate a list of measures that have particular application in their own environment. This should involve some training in dealing fairly with older workers and removing hurdles to their motivation. In earlier chapters, we brought forth a clear and unequivocal message about the emerging labor markets. That message needs to be understood and communicated forcefully.

To test your personal level of motivation to achieve, we enclose as Exhibit 8.4 a little questionnaire to be answered and scored in accordance with the instructions.

EXHIBIT 8.4: Testing Your Motivation to Achieve

As an older worker, at times you may believe that your drive to achieve has weakened, that job success is impossible or meaningless, and that challenges and rewards are reserved for your younger colleagues. Why not test your own motivation to achieve? (Give yourself 3 points for high, 2 points for average, 1 point for low motivation.)

Qualities That Show High Motivation to Achieve	*Your Own Assessment*
1. Being effective and influential in your work	_____
2. Being quite active	_____
3. Being future-oriented	_____
4. Wanting to take personal responsibility	_____
5. Willing to take risk	_____
6. Wanting honest feedback on results	_____
7. Taking pride in your accomplishments	_____

Reaching a score of 18 points would clearly demonstrate high motivation to achieve, while even a score of 15 points (moderate motivation) should dissipate any of your concerns that job success, the ability to handle challenges, and personal growth are no longer possible.

CHAPTER 9

Appraising Older Employee Performance

How can an organization be managed so as to ensure age fairness to all its employees? How can the rights of older employees be protected without infringing on the rights of other age groups? Even an organization that is doing everything possible to avoid age discrimination in employment can take many additional steps to ensure a productive and viable workplace with a culture and climate that promote age cooperation and harmony. A defensive legal posture may be necessary at times, but it is still a primary managerial responsibility to ensure that standards for employee performance and productivity meet the interests of both the employee and the organization. This means both practicing age-neutral employment actions and seeking out the challenges and opportunities inherent in a multigenerational organization.

MANAGING PERFORMANCE

Since not every older employee produces adequately, decisions must be made when an employee does not meet the organization's standards. The task then is to deal with the older employee as an individual rather than as a statistic and to resolve each productivity issue as fairly as possible. A useful procedure for dealing with unsatisfactory performance is to:

- Define the gap between the job requirements and the person's output in terms as measurable as possible.
- Determine the cause (insofar as possible).
- Decide whether or not it appears to be a temporary problem (as with an illness).
- Inform the person of the discrepancy between performance and the standards.
- Mutually plan for, and work toward, a satisfactory resolution. Ideally, this means helping the employee to close the gap between job requirements and output—to be successful on the job. Generating an imaginative win-win outcome reflects managerial competence.

If the cooperative approach fails to close the productivity gap, disciplinary action and possibly termination procedures may be necessary. With older workers in particular, the emphasis should be on resolving the problem of unsatisfactory performance to avoid violating the legal constraints of the Age Discrimination in Employment Act (ADEA) regarding discipline and termination. General guidelines for taking fair and legal actions require that:

1. Performance standards are clearly established.
2. Each employee's output is monitored and measured, in some verifiable fashion, against the job standards.
3. All employees doing similar work are evaluated according to the same standards.
4. The gap between job requirements and the employee's performance is clearly documented and communicated to the employee.
5. There are no factors such as faulty equipment or unsafe working conditions that may adversely affect the employee's performance.
6. Reasonable efforts have been made by the organization and its management to help the employee correct the performance problem.
7. All aspects of the employee's performance, including absences,

have been documented, and the documentation shows fairness and an age-neutral approach.

8. Such documentation does not begin when the employee files a grievance but is undertaken as soon as performance becomes unsatisfactory.

This performance-based approach generally makes certain that age itself is not a factor in the adverse action—that output or service is the only issue. When undertaken correctly and convincingly, the adverse action becomes merely an expression of the organization's legitimate right to get the job done well. The above guidelines can, and should, be applied humanely and fairly to all employees.

This approach does not mean favored treatment for the elderly; rather, it means establishing realistic job criteria that must be met and then evaluating each person's ability to perform that job as fairly as possible. If older people have physical infirmities that would prevent them from performing the work at hand without special equipment, for example, they should be treated as any other handicapped people would be, with the provision of reasonable accommodations, and not punished for being older.

As employment decisions in such areas as promotion, training, and discharge are increasingly challenged in the courts, the basis for such employer actions needs to be called into account. The key question is whether the individual was being judged on the basis of performance or of some other, more suspect criteria. Organizations that have solid performance measures that are communicated and fairly applied to all employees tend to be in a far more viable position than those that do not. Unfortunately, many performance appraisal systems are deficient in provable standards and are all too often inconsistently applied. Where age could be a factor in a dispute over a personnel action, weakness in the performance appraisal leaves the organization and its managers vulnerable.

Creating an effective and clearly verifiable performance appraisal system and using it as a primary basis for all personnel decisions are certainly a tough task. To get supervisors, personnel specialists, and managers at all levels to then use that appraisal system consistently is an even greater challenge. The following sections discuss some of the primary aspects considered by experts to be the basis of a solid performance appraisal system.

The employer's performance appraisal system is by far the most crucial element in a defense against a charge of age discrimination. To be an effective tool in such litigation, the procedure used in evaluating employees should involve clear criteria that are consistently applied to all employees. If possible, it is best to follow some standardized model of evaluation, such as that published by the American Management Association.

Under the ADEA, the employee has the initial burden of proof to establish a "prima facie" case of age discrimination. In general, the employee must demonstrate the following elements to establish such a case:

- Membership in the protected group.
- Discipline, discharge, or failure to receive a promotion.
- Previous or present ability to do the job.

Once evidence is presented to this effect, the burden is on the employer to offer rebuttal arguments. This is best done by showing an objective, fairly applied, and regularly administered system of performance evaluation for all employees doing similar work.

While the courts have not required that employers maintain a highly formalized appraisal procedure, evidence of such a system does carry substantial weight with the courts. Generally, the courts seek three characteristics in performance appraisals: reasonableness, reliability, and relevancy. The first characteristic applies to the method's acceptability to its users. The system should have a clearly stated purpose and should have fairness and objectivity as its goal. Second, the evaluation technique is deemed reliable if appraisals of the same individual are "consistent among different raters and over a period of time. They should contain a minimum of subjectivity that leads to distortion." Finally, the system should be evaluating only those aspects of the work that are necessary to the successful performance of the job. "Personality traits, race, sex and age are rarely relevant to job performance."

To achieve an appraisal procedure that is reasonable, reliable, and relevant, management should, at a minimum, review its job descriptions to ensure that they are nondiscriminatory as well as specific. They should include descriptions of basic activities or roles required in the job and in other similar positions; special activities required that are unique to a given location, process, project, technical requirement, and so on; identifiable or measurable output, products, or services resulting from performance; and skills, abilities, and knowledge actually necessary for successful performance (specifying skills, general knowledge, years of schooling, or academic degrees that are not clearly related to the job performance may not be adequate proof).

One authority suggests that if performance becomes an issue, "rarely should a standardized [performance appraisal] form be simply checked or circled. . . . Supervisors should be required to provide a written narrative comment, including specific reference to performance deficiencies during the period under evaluation. . . . Supervisors should be trained to write appraisals as objective reports of *performance* not as rewards or concessions. If an evaluated position lends itself to quantitative measurement the measurement should be made and included in the evaluation."[1]

The organization should, in addition, offer extensive training to supervisors and others in all aspects of the performance appraisal system, including its objectives and means of implementation. Some companies conduct mock evaluation sessions to develop appraisal-counseling skills that are taped and then discussed with the supervisors. It is crucial that supervisors understand the importance of administering the program regularly and in a manner consistent with that of their colleagues. As is common practice in larger organizations, employees should be evaluated at least once a year, and the evaluation report should be retained for three or more years. Again, such appraisals should be in writing.

In each of the major personnel actions—promotions, layoffs, and discharges—the employer is required to present counterevidence when confronted with a charge of age discrimination. The consistently well documented performance evaluation offers the best means of making the argument. For example, when an older employee is passed over for a promotion, the employer must show that the complaining employee was not as qualified as the candidate selected. Here, it is not the employee's performance in his or her present job that is the principal criterion but rather the employee's potential performance relative to that of other employees. With respect to layoffs, the employer is required to demonstrate that the laid-off employee was not as qualified or tenured as those selected to remain. Finally, defending an outright discharge involves more than simply showing that the employee was performing at a minimally acceptable level. This type of personnel action probably requires a further demonstration by the employer that the decision was nondiscriminatory.

How important is performance appraisal if push comes to shove on an issue of the performance of any older employee? *Gill* v. *Union Carbide, Inc.*,[2] is a good case example of the kind of impact an effective appraisal system can have. *Gill* involved an allegation of age discrimination by four discharged employees. In finding for the company, the court cited three characteristics of the appraisal system that it believed upheld the company's argument that it was nondiscriminatory:

1. The evaluation procedures related logically to the work being done.
2. The system was regularly implemented without favor to any particular group.
3. The workers had been informed of the appraisal method.

In contrast, a termination suit involving General Motors shows how local management's failure to fairly evaluate an employee's performance can backfire. One year before he was fired, the employee was given the highest possible rating. But six days after his termination his former boss assigned him the second lowest of six possible ratings. The company lost the suit.

In summary, in most ADEA cases where the employer has prevailed, the combination of a regularly administered, written appraisal system and the credible testimony of the supervisor has tipped the scales in the employer's favor. Alternatively, cases where the employee has won have been characterized by a poorly documented system and noncredible supervisory testimony.

Overall, a good performance appraisal system—one that actually measures an employee's contribution to meeting specific and fair organizational needs—by its nature, contributes substantially to age-neutral human resource management.

SUPERVISOR READINESS

Almost any aspect of older people's work life can be enhanced if their supervisor is ready, willing, and able to act. Most are willing, but some, it seems, are lacking in the areas of being ready and able.

Because of ineffective management practices, some supervisors allow themselves to be overwhelmed and consequently become burned out, tired, and unmotivated to make any special effort. This is despite the fact that many older, highly experienced people are available to help share the load. The common belief of supervisors that they should do everything themselves wears them out and defeats them. They then become angry when called on to do more, which gets in the way of their objectivity, saps more energy, and turns their outlook even more negative. If they were to relax, see the older person as an opportunity rather than a problem, and begin to think about, and search for, positive features, they might regain the equanimity required to solve any personnel problem that they encounter.

Two other problems may afflict the supervisor: concentration on an older employee's negative attributes and a general reluctance to believe that older people can succeed. Long-standing prejudice and age bias can often be overcome if everyone focuses on the true advantages of age. The thoughts of psychologist Carl Jung are appropriate here. He noticed that "after life's mid-point, people may develop their previously neglected, less rational [creative] side for a new meaning. It is precisely this late development of instinct and the subconscious that, superimposed on earlier experience, sharpens judgment and understanding." For a supervisor to fail to stress this positive potential is self-defeating.

Finally, much has been written not about the fear of failure but about a fear of success that is within our reach. To many, this may sound strange, since we are often preoccupied by a fear of failing. But the other side of the coin, a fear of winning really big, is more subtle and harder to pin down, though just as invidious. Why do people back off from opportunity, retreat when winning, and have vague premonitions of disaster when things are going well? Success at a high level may not match people's self-image and may therefore lead to discomfort when they start to "get too big for their britches." Unless these issues of success are dealt with, many supervisors—and consequently their older employees—may never get to enjoy the greater fruits of their labors and abilities.

GUIDELINES TO PREVENT CHARGES OF AGE DISCRIMINATION

The following guidelines offer an overview of the suggestions made in the literature for avoiding any indication or charge of age discrimination:

1. The concept of age neutrality should be built into all phases of personnel and management policies. For example, decisions regarding promotions and training for the older employee should be made in the same manner as they are for any other worker, regardless of how close the employer believes the worker is to retirement. This ensures that older workers have access to career opportunities consistent with their aspirations, abilities, and potential.
2. As a general rule, managers should be made aware of the provisions of the ADEA and should stay up-to-date regarding developments in the act. Some suggest that supervisors review such sources as the "ADEA Update" of the General Counsel for the National Commission on Aging, which appears frequently in the journal *Aging and Work*. In addition, managers should be familiar with their own state's age-discrimination laws.
3. Supervisory personnel should be sensitized to the fact that any deprecatory age-related remarks, made in either a formal or an informal setting, may set up the organization for a lawsuit or weaken its position in such a suit. While most managers are aware that age references cannot be made in, for example, job

advertisements or performance appraisals, many do not pay as much attention to casual references in internal memos or offhand remarks.

4. It is important as well that personnel departments establish and document a track record of disseminating frequent and widespread information about the organization's antidiscrimination policies. If an age-discrimination lawsuit is filed, courts tend to look favorably on evidence of a long-standing organizational policy of nondiscrimination and may assess any damages accordingly.

5. An employer may want to consider placing qualified older workers in personnel positions to serve as watchdogs, trainers, or facilitators of ADEA goals.

6. If an employer believes that a certain job cannot be successfully performed by workers over a certain age, concrete documentation to support this decision should be available. In most cases, it is better to "performance test" each employee's abilities rather than establishing a hiring cutoff based on age.

7. Using written tests as a hiring criterion is often risky. Such test material may not correlate with job requirements; more importantly, results of such tests are usually inadequate as predictors of job performance.

8. Employers should periodically review the age of their employees on a unit-by-unit basis to determine whether older workers are adequately represented. This information can provide good statistical evidence if the employer can show that such representation has been achieved.

9. Since, as discussed earlier, most ADEA lawsuits involve allegations of unfair terminations, the work performance of a replacement employee should soon be measurably superior to that of the former incumbent. As always, the performance differences between the two employees should be carefully recorded.

10. If an employee is transferred or offered a demotion in lieu of being laid off or fired, the reasons for this, too, should be documented so that no argument can be made that an employment alternative was not offered.

11. If a discharge is unavoidable, the employer should first consider the possibility of a voluntary retirement or resignation, if necessary

based on certain inducements to be offered to the employee. In such an event, the employee should be requested, without pressure, to sign a waiver stating that the retirement or resignation is, in fact, voluntary and that he or she has no further claims against the organization. The wording of such a waiver should be reviewed with an attorney.

12. When any disciplinary action is taken, the supervisor should be able to point to some progressive disciplinary system whose guidelines are known to employees and are fairly applied. Such a system typically involves such provisions as "an oral warning for the first offense, a written warning for the second, suspension for the third, and termination for the fourth." At each step, the action should be documented and discussed with the employee, and the employee should be given an opportunity to correct his or her behavior.

13. To further reduce the need for legal action, the employer may wish to consider resolving employee–employer problems through an internal grievance and arbitration mechanism. Besides the obvious savings of litigation costs, another important advantage for the employer is that an arbitrator, rather than a jury, will hear the case and that the arbitration process usually involves several steps aimed at resolving the issue.

14. Employers should be aware that employment actions directed at management-level employees should be just as age-neutral as those aimed at other workers. According to the U.S. House Select Committee on Aging, managers and supervisors are the most likely victims of age discrimination.

15. Employers should also take note that a notice regarding the ADEA law must be posted in an obvious spot in every organization, employment agency, or union hall covered by the act. Lawsuits have been lost because of the employer's failure to post this notice.

The very fact of consciously applying some or all of these guidelines as organizational policy creates heightened awareness of ADEA issues in the organization and indicates that the organization is taking a proactive approach to age neutrality and fairness.

CREATING AN AGE-FAIR EMPLOYMENT CLIMATE

In summary, the primary methods for creating an age-fair employment climate in the workplace are the following:

1. Revising policies and procedures to make them age-neutral
2. Training supervisors and managers in the rights and protections of the ADEA and how to handle age problems on the basis of good management practices, free of personal biases and assumptions
3. Developing uniform standards of performance and behavior
4. Striving for objective performance measures
5. Focusing organizational attention on the productive contributions that can be made by older employees
6. Striving to reconcile age-related differences between older and younger employees
7. Balancing the age-attribute scale by taking advantage of the special characteristics of older employees—their experience, insight, stability, and loyalty—and giving fair attention to these special attributes

Training supervisory and management personnel in ADEA requirements and appropriate responses is critical. They should not be left to guess at appropriate forms of behavior. Today, the ultimate logic of managing well is the antidote to possible ADEA problems. But more important perhaps is the sense of organizational justice that these actions can produce.

As an addendum to this chapter and as a *real-life perspective*, we have described and summarized the new performance appraisal system for most of its civilian personnel of the U.S. Coast Guard. This new system and the circumstances of its introduction were covered in much detail in our earlier book, *New Corporate Cultures That Motivate*. It is a surprising account of the culture of a large military service organization and of an employee initiative that brought considerable change to the way the government operates. This example may be helpful to organizations looking for ways to make the evaluation of employee performance more effective.

Establishing a New Performance Management
System at the U.S. Coast Guard

In the late 1990s, the U.S. Coast Guard (USCG) created a new performance management system, known under the acronym of EARS for *E*xcellence, *A*chievement, and *R*ecognition *S*ystem, covering most of its civilian personnel. EARS is now in full operation.

When such a system is introduced, which can affect a person's pay, you are likely (almost certain) to encounter apathy at best, reservations in some quarters, and often resistance in others. This new system was to alter the conditions for over 7,500 people. Important as the new system was, the greatest impact came from the way it was developed, particularly in a government agency. Typically, to design or modify such a system, personnel experts would adapt a "rational system" largely reliant on what was known about such systems from other organizations and from the general literature in the field. To its users, "the system" would have been regarded as more of the same, which in effect it would have been.

However, the approach the USCG used largely disproved the connotation that "people naturally resist change." In reality people resist change that they perceive as threatening or as holding no discernible benefit to them. Instead, the USCG's developmental process stressed openness and ensured user involvement, understanding of the details, and support of the main features, from the beginning and every step of the way.

The rationale behind developing a new system rested on changes in national policies concerning personnel management, which called for results-based performance, the need to promote more effective communications throughout the organization, performance feedback, and linking individual performance to organizational outcomes. While the former problems persist in the mega-organization of Homeland Security, created after September 11, 2001, the USCG has been able to maintain its own system of effectively relating pay to individual performance, which makes it an effective model for similar organizations.

DEFINING THE PROBLEM AND DEVELOPING AN ANSWER

The key players in this effort created four teams:

- A design team
- An events planning team
- A marketing and implementation team
- A rewards and recognition team

The EARS system emphasized strong, two-way communications between supervisors/managers and their employees. It also stressed accountability and joint ownership of performance goals and outcomes, provided meaningful recognition and rewards, and fostered a learning environment that challenged and motivated employees.

The design team developed a unique policy that created a "new way of doing business" for the USCG. The design was essentially customer-based by inviting nontechnical "clients" to join the team (versus using only personnel experts). They wanted to encourage people to suggest design options, given all opportunities, and to develop different strategic possibilities rather than focus on technical details of the design. This led to a fresh and creative approach rather than "more of the same." Many of the participating users later commented that they had never seen such a customer-focused effort in a government agency.

At the leadership level, a guidance team of key military and civilian personnel people was created to champion and steer the EARS effort. Their primary responsibility was to offer advice and to help market the program throughout the organization as it developed.

DESIGNING THE SYSTEM

Creating a customer focus was a major part of the design effort. For example, only four of the ten members of the design team were "personnelists" with the aim to provide insight and experience in broadly understanding goals and needs of the new system. The other six members were future customers, representing the microcosm of the USCG and including employees, supervisors, and managers; people from the field and from headquarters; and people from all different occupations, grades, and pay plans.

It soon became clear that more customer input was needed to make the system more client-responsive. The best way seemed to be bringing together focus groups to gather more ideas and input. With a total of seven focus group meetings across the country, the design group was able to bring over 300 civilian and military employees and supervisors together. As the focus groups represented a cross-section of the different factions of the USCG and included both military and civilian personnel, it was possible to model the new system to the realities of their workplace—a significant factor in the success for EARS.

Part of the success of the design team was also that proposals were rarely voted on. Rather, the team tried to look for different and more creative options; finding win-win solutions; and reaching consensus. Sensitive issues in the technical or legal area were worked out by the specialists, leaving the design firm and without a need for significant changes.

Four common ideas emerged from the customer feedback:

- *Appraisals.* There was a definite need expressed for a simplified, more flexible, and fair system that makes supervisors responsible for effective performance management.
- *Setting goals.* Customers felt that clear goals and directions encourage employee buy-in and should be linked to the job and customer needs.
- *Communication and feedback.* Feedback on performance should be job-specific, continuous, timely, and documented. Effective communication between supervisor and employee is critical.
- *Employee development.* Training and developmental programs with emphasis on individual development plans should be offered and adequately funded, with an added focus on cross-training and career growth opportunities.

EVENTS PLANNING

A special team was responsible for planning the EARS orientation blitz. The training approach with the aim to obtain the workforce's buy-in was to cover military and civilian employees at small and large sites throughout the country—a truly Herculean task!

MARKETING AND IMPLEMENTATION

Marketing the system openly—rather than shrouding it in secrecy, as is customary in command-and-control organizations—began virtually at its inception. The use of decision-making teams, and the intentional seeking out of advice, information, and ideas from the employee level made a great difference in organizational openness.

Employee participation was the key component of the EARS marketing plan. Throughout the process, practically everyone was kept informed of developments and results as well as invited to submit questions about the evolving system. A monthly newsletter addressed employee questions, announced training sessions, and publicized key events.

The inclusive nature of this process may have seemed strange to many at first but was gradually embraced by all personnel. Including people such as a union steward on the design team, as well as the broad variety of employees in the focus groups, sent a clear message that this time something was different. The EARS program signaled the advent of a new and more inclusive culture at the USCG.

In the implementation phase, more than 3,000 people who would have to conduct performance appraisals were trained in the new approach. This helped ensure that the new system would be consistently and fairly applied. In time, the USCG system became a model for other government agencies. As an ancillary benefit, the EARS process improved the relationship between USCG leadership and its two major unions. All in all, EARS laid the foundation for a more powerful, adaptable, and inclusive place to work.

PART III

THE OLDER WORKER AS PART OF TODAY'S MULTIGENERATIONAL WORKPLACE

At the end of our journey through the issues of older employees, we would like to look at the needs and possibilities to make the older worker's role and place in today's multigenerational society successful. This hinges on several issues and factors critical to job success, for example:

- *Ensuring job success for the older employee.* The supervisor's guidance continues to be important. Her or his role may have changed from the former command-and-control mode to one of providing expertise, support, and help so much needed by the average older person on the job. Yet historically and again today the influence of the supervisor at the workplace is crucial for any employee.

- *Developing productive work teams.* This will increasingly be an important responsibility in the new multigenerational organization. In the past, we have seen a lot of strife and resentment between old and young in work groups and teams, but today this seems to have changed. Both old and young have a somewhat different perspective of the workplace, but we seem to see much intergenerational cooperation emerging.

- *Overcoming low individual and work group productivity.* The reasons for productivity problems can be manifold, like age bias and discriminative attitudes on the part of some group members; job withdrawal or anxiety on the part of the older worker; being afraid to admit to a lack of familiarity with certain issues; or being fearful of making mistakes and losing face. The solution to this problem rests on both sides—a definite encouragement by the supervisor and the worker's peers as well as enthusiasm and a positive attitude by the older worker.

- *Creating alternative work programs and flexible benefits for older employees.* This chapter covers the whole realm of possibilities and brings many examples of the creativeness of certain organizations to keep the older worker connected with the workplace. With today's demographic developments, however, many older workers will be needed part- or full-time anyway and may want to continue in their jobs on that basis, which makes the need for special programs somewhat less urgent.

The final chapter of the book, entitled "Keeping Pace with Changes in the Workforce," we start by providing a little summary of the different guideposts of our journey. Then we move on to highlight seven significant themes that we think will stay in the forefront of the older workers issue for years to come. This is intended to give the reader additional food for thought, maybe as an incentive and encouragement to make use of, and promote, *the older worker advantage*, so important for the future of our society, economy, and work community.

CHAPTER 10

Ensuring Job Success for the Older Employee

Historically, an employee's supervisor has been the critical factor for job success. This is still true in today's workplace, even where the role of supervisors has changed significantly. They are expected to be more like leaders, setting examples for their people and providing needed guidance and expertise. In that sense, older workers depend a lot on their relationship to the supervisor in order to allow updating of their skills and to ensure productive synergies with coworkers. In other words, supervisory leadership continues to be critical for the job success of each older employee.

The supervisor's job has been described as getting the work done through other people, effectively applying the organization's policies and procedures, and, more recently, providing support and expertise so that the objectives are met. These views assume that the supervisor will operate within the law and other constraints placed on the organization by society. In our context, it includes having a firm grasp of the organization's responsibilities and its policies regarding the treatment of older employees. The first-line supervisor is on the firing line in applying such policies, and therefore the quality of the supervisor's leadership is important.

Worker productivity in our Knowledge Society, where output is not easily measured, is often determined by how employees feel about their job, their employer, their coworkers, and so on—in short, their level of morale and motivation. As we saw earlier, the supervisor's behavior is critical in these areas. Ample evidence indicates that older people want to be treated as an important part of their work or peer group. They want to contribute and be accepted, and they want to feel secure and be treated fairly. At the same time—and that should come as no surprise—they want to be recognized for their knowledge and past accomplishments. Again, they are looking for real challenges that are a reach but within their capabilities, and they want to be listened to when they have a suggestion or a recommendation based on their experience or particular perception.

An effective supervisor treats employees similarly when it comes to the issues of fairness and equal opportunity and applies required rules and procedures without distinction. However, as a real leader of people, he or she considers the special needs of all employees, their unique qualifications or strengths, and special situational factors as they arise. Successful supervisors pay ample attention to each of their people to recognize special needs, opportunities, and problems. They step in and invest time and effort to help resolve any difficulty, no matter what the age of the employee involved.

GETTING THE JOB DONE

Because of the massive downsizing and the concurrent elimination of management layers in many of our largest organizations since the mid-1980s, the role of the supervisor has tended to become a bottom-up support of the work group rather than traditional top-down control.

In today's workplace, excellent supervisors are sensitive to the talents, experience, and creative ideas of their people. They try to integrate special skills and abilities that each one of their employees possesses into the work of their group. They strive to maximize each individual's contributions over the short and the long term.

Unfortunately, the immediacy of the first-line supervisor's responsibilities—that is, the concern for today's output, keeping on schedule, and getting a myriad of things accomplished—often leads to the kind of myopia that can be injurious to older workers' needs. Consequently, many supervisors come to ignore older employees and fail to foster their learning and development. As an antidote to such oversight, a series of questions may be put forth, such as these:

- If a challenging project or assignment comes up, involving a considerable learning effort for the recipient, would I give it to a younger or an older employee?

- If an opportunity for advancement arose in another department and I were asked for my recommendation as to a suitable candidate, would I tend to give the nod to a younger person because I assume he or she will be around longer?

- If there were an opening for one of my people to attend an advanced seminar, would I be tempted to send the younger person rather than an older one, even though their expertise and merit levels were similar?

Research clearly indicates that many supervisors tend to favor the younger person, not necessarily because of age prejudice and stereotyping but because they felt that promoting the interest of the younger employee was the right thing to do for the organization. The result is what we know—generations of older employees see their future dead-ended, their jobs repetitious and uninspiring, and their advancement opportunities truncated. An effective supervisor tries to balance fairly the distribution of opportunities and helps older workers to rekindle their interest in self-development. This goes far in bringing back the excitement about their job and the belief that their future holds promise.

THE SUPERVISOR'S ROLE AND RESPONSIBILITY

First-line supervisors also provide the first line of fairness and equal opportunity between the employee and the organization. They are the critical link in representing the spirit and the culture of an organization to the employees as well as the ideas and expectations of the employees to the organization. This role of supervisors requires that they must know a great deal about the organization and its history, as well as its plans and policies, in order to be able to convey and interpret them to the employees. This helps the employees to gain a better understanding of where their jobs fit into the greater picture and to make correct assumptions and decisions in the context of organizational goals.

With the advent of the twenty-first century, the role of the supervisor has become more complex because he or she needs to be better informed and equipped to make successful business decisions. Supervisors not only have to lead and support an increasingly demanding, multigenerational workforce but need more complex skills for decision making, financial analysis, and computer and Internet use, as well as coaching and employee development. Let's look at some of these skills and how they refer to older workers in particular[1]:

- *Communications.* While the organization may adhere to a philosophy of minimal communications, the supervisor should practice "open book management" with his or her team. Information about competitors, market developments, or new techniques for cost reduction or quality enhancement may be useful resources, where often the older team members may have relevant knowledge and experience.

- *Team-building.* Today's supervisor is faced with a diversity of people of different ages, races, gender, and ethnic backgrounds. It's an important task to make use of these different experience levels, work styles, and other backgrounds and develop the right synergy among them. It's crucial to fit the different pieces into the puzzle of the work projects. Obviously, this is particularly important for the older employee who wants to be a full member of the team.

- *Skill development.* In order to be an effective coach and mentor for the team, supervisors have to keep abreast of new developments and technological advances that affect the team's work effort. They have to make sure that skills are updated and learning challenges are given to the people who need them the most. The access to training opportunities is often quite motivational, as are "one-day sabbaticals." In this particular area, a challenging opportunity for older workers may be to mentor younger or newly hired employees until they have reached the right skill level.

- *Keeping score.* This is a new and important function of supervisors, although it is meant to be supportive rather than controlling. It is up to them to provide the team with results of their efforts, both as to output and quality; to measure performance against plan and prior periods; and with all that to create a sense of ownership and recognition. For the older employee, it is of much importance to be part and parcel of the score keeping, receiving the same degree of recognition and communication as the rest of the team.

- *Reporting to senior management.* Often, the supervisor gets squeezed in between the ideas of senior management and the suggestions of his or her team. It's important that the supervisor's viewpoint and arguments be supported by hard facts and the knowledge of the overall situation. Obtaining merit pool increases, personal recognition of senior management of a particular success, or the nod for special training opportunities goes far in supporting morale and motivation of the team.

These skill areas highlight some of the complexities of today's workplace. All in all, supervisors have to be able to create a work environment that makes team members and, among them, the older employees ready to work hard and to make a difference.

THE ISSUE OF AGE DISCRIMINATION

The job of the supervisor in protecting the organization against age-bias litigation and related problems rests not only on observing policies and regulations that deal with age discrimination but more importantly on carefully documenting any disciplinary action, on being reasonable and fair in conducting performance appraisals, and on handling consistently all personnel actions like training, leaves, transfers, and promotions. "No need to worry," you might say, "I'm not prejudiced about age." Such may well be the case—surveys of management personnel mostly indicate that few people consider themselves biased with respect to age. However, it is nevertheless a difficult subject matter to teach and learn. In subtle and sometimes hardly noticeable ways, discrimination happens all the time, and it is likely that we all do it. Subsequently, we rationalize it beautifully.

The difficulty faced by any supervisor is clear: while they may have sound standards for making personnel decisions, based on such factors as technical competence, skills, and experience, research suggests that there may be *unconscious* standards as well, such as the employee's age. This particular standard may well be outside the supervisor's awareness but is grounded in unconscious beliefs about the inability of older workers to perform as well as their younger peers in assignments that demand flexibility, creativity, and a high degree of motivation.

One of the most powerful aspects of this research is that participants, when asked for their opinions on organizational policies regarding older employees, favored more aggressive affirmative action goals as to retirement and vesting schedules. This clearly suggests that the differential treatment of older and younger team members was not a conscious discrimination but the result of unconscious stereotyping. Because it is not that visible and operates at a very low level of awareness, stereotyping is a much harder nut to crack than discrimination.

Finally, it may at times be necessary for the supervisor to confront higher-level managers in circumstances where their behavior or direction is contrary to the organizational policies and responsibilities—risky as that confrontation may be. As we said before, in age discrimination and the pertinent litigation, the supervisor represents the first line of accountability between the employee and the organization.

SAFETY AND PRODUCTIVITY

Supervisors generally know more about the state of the workplace under their control than any other member of management. For that reason, it's an important supervisory responsibility to maintain a safe workplace and to provide for the welfare of older employees. While the supervisor is responsible for all employees, the knowledge of particular vulnerabilities or special risks for older workers is helpful.

While—as we mentioned in an earlier chapter—it has been established that occupational injuries occur at a lower rate among older employees than among younger ones, older workers do get hurt and often more severely and with more cost to the organization in terms of lost time and compensation payments. Consequently, a supervisor may consider a lesser load of heavy stress and physical strain in the job assignments of older workers, appraising not only the person's age but also the individual capability. Such considerations reflect sound management and proper handling of human resources, rather than implying some form of reverse discrimination.

The same kind of reasoning may apply to other age groups with particular strengths and weaknesses. Being sensitive to, and aware of, the particular abilities and special needs of certain individuals enables the supervisor to allocate time and effort to where the payoff in health and safety will be greatest.

SUPERVISORY ENCOURAGEMENT AND SUPPORT

As mentioned before, motivation is an inner process that cannot easily be induced from the outside. However, the supervisor is not helpless to influence it. She or he can offer incentives, recognize and reward achievements, provide help and assistance when needed, create opportunities and challenges, foster a climate for ideas and suggestions, and share information with employees. This applies to all employees regardless of age.

When it comes to older workers, there are some general thoughts, outlined below, that may be of interest and guidance to supervisors. They are offered with a note of caution because individual situations may vary and the approach may have to be adapted accordingly.

Older employees often do not get as much positive reinforcement, encouragement, and recognition as others. Yet this type of attention is a basic human need and is valued at any age for good self-image and mental health. Older employees may have a greater need for praise and recognition because of diminishing numbers of friends and family in their lives. With the loosening of traditional family ties, older workers become more dependent on their peers and on their supervisor. The social aspect of their job becomes ever more important.

Older employees value opportunities and challenges as much as anyone else if they feel they are prepared for them and can handle them. If they cannot maintain and update their skills, their sense of self and their mastery of the work suffer and deteriorate. Being useful and effective in their job can provide older workers with a feeling of joy and satisfaction. Pride and achievement are of particular value to older workers.

The midcareer or midlife crisis may lead to a shift in values. Without new challenges and continued investment in personal skills, people start seeing themselves as stuck or plateaued and consequently develop negative behaviors that affect others as well as themselves. In those circumstances, it is important to redefine success away from a purely financial yardstick. New values and a more positive attitude and view of life lead to a different level of morale and motivation. The supervisor can be an important catalyst for that development.

AGE DIFFERENCES BETWEEN EMPLOYEE AND SUPERVISOR

Most of us have been raised to expect that older people will have some authority over us, and many of us have been ingrained with well-defined notions of our role with respect to older people. The results of this early programming range from a sense of respect to a rather general notion that older people have some advantages that we cannot yet claim. We comfort ourselves with the thought that "one day we'll be big and the world will be ours."

Sometimes, this conditioning and the feelings it evokes cause a supervisor to be uncomfortable giving directions to an older employee. With the advent of the baby boomers and with the unrestrained self-confidence and technological arrogance they sometimes exude, the inverse may also be true—older supervisors may feel inhibited to "manage" their younger employees. Some of this discomfort may be overcome by strictly focusing on the person's performance rather than on the person.

Age problems can involve goals and expectations, ideals, and values, as well as work habits and operating styles. For some younger supervisors, appraising the work of their seniors and communicating performance deficiencies to an older worker may become difficult. Also, some sociologists claim that how we interact with another person depends on how we perceive that other person's status relative to our own. In an organization, this status conflict involves not only age but also seniority on the job, level of position and accomplishment, and even relative incomes.

There are some helpful approaches to solving this sort of age dilemma. Supervisors can learn to be less threatening in confrontation, to listen without immediately evaluating, and to creatively solve performance problems with older employees by identifying common goals. This may require that the supervisor see the older employee as a person with certain needs rather than simply as one who is older. The older employee may need appreciation for good work and the opportunity for achievement. Effective feedback, in particular if it is negative, should be based on factual information. Once the problem is clear, mutual problem solving can start.

Criticism is evaluative and judgmental and, as such, threatening. It therefore evokes instinctive resistance rather than cooperation, since our *primary* human needs include survival and security. Criticism is particularly threatening to someone who feels bypassed by events and is not highly regarded. Information, on the other hand, is merely factual, and though it may be interpreted any way the recipient chooses, it is far less likely to be threatening. This is further helped by an offer to assist in closing the gap between performance and goal expectation. A cooperative problem-solving approach means being forward-looking rather than wallowing in what is past, which cannot be changed anyway. Older employees, in particular, need the supervisor's support in looking forward to a new challenge and a more hopeful day.

LEADERSHIP BY EXAMPLE

Today's supervisors are expected to place their willingness to support and to counsel ahead of their managerial function of giving directions. Their priorities are to serve people's individual needs, to establish trust among them, and to maintain consistent values. They should be role models of responsible and ethical behavior. At the same time, the need for people's growth, providing opportunities for challenge and learning, letting people enjoy the "fun" of making decisions and experience the camaraderie of a work team should be dear to their heart. This is what supervisory leadership is all about.

Some questions to consider when looking at your own organization:

- The role of the supervisor has changed from top-down command-and-control in the Industrial Age to one of bottom-up support, guidance, and expertise in today's Knowledge Society. Can you confirm this observation in your own organization?

- In many ways, older workers depend on their supervisor for becoming full members of multigenerational teams, for maintaining and developing their skills, and for making full use of their experience and knowledge to the benefit of the organization. In your own workplace, is the environment adequate for older individuals, or should certain improvements be made?

- Discrimination in any form is a difficult issue and often grounded in unconscious beliefs. What are your own opinions and principles regarding older coworkers?

CHAPTER 11

Developing Productive Work Teams

Supervisors and managers in business, government, and institutions have long talked about "my team," "team effort," and "team players," but off the athletic field real team play seems scarce and elusive. The traditional hierarchical structure with its lines of authority and chain of command still dominates the thinking and behavior of many managers and quite a few employees. Culturally, many people still see boxes on our organizational charts with lines of authority running to sub-subboxes and so on. This mental model of how organizations function is still so pervasive that even when we consciously set out to build teams and teamwork, we often do it badly.

Certain studies have found that over 65% of the communication within groups took place between individual workers and their supervisors (up and down), and only 35% laterally between group members.[1] Yet it appears certain that in our society we increasingly need to work in teams of various sorts. As workplace problems become more technologically complex and interdisciplinary and as the various kinds of knowledge and expertise possessed by individuals need to be integrated creatively, we must focus more effectively on team efforts. However, it is exactly here that older employees in general present both a serious obstacle to team development and an unparalleled opportunity.

The work teams emerging are not just collections of people reporting to their supervisors or the occasional committees of the past. A half century ago, the hierarchical organizational structures began to crumble in the high-tech industries, with informal networking, task-force teams, and ad hoc groups being used to solve problems where answers to increasingly complex challenges were needed more quickly than the traditional organization could provide them.

New and more complex forms of work teams are increasingly appearing. The use of interdisciplinary study teams, management-labor committees, self-directed work groups, task forces, participative decision-making efforts, and new types of organizational tools is shifting much of the focus in organizations from individual contributions to group activity. The question before us here, then, is, Does age make a difference in meeting our need for cooperative work-group efforts, and if so, how can we maximize the contribution of older employees?

AGE AND GROUP WORK

Is there a generational problem for older employees in performing some types of work in groups? Observations of the effect of member age on the work of homogeneous age groups show some mixed results. Several studies and reports indicate that cooperative behavior in groups produces more effective performance than individual effort. Tying this together with another common observation—that young people today tend to be more cooperative and less competitive than earlier generations—is intriguing.

In one study participants were given a task to perform individually and then put into homogeneous age- and status-related groups and asked to perform a pretested second task, of equal complexity and difficulty, in the group setting. The results bore out earlier findings that groups scored more highly than individuals. But more important here was the finding that younger groups scored better than older groups and did so because they were better able to draw on the performance of their "best" (or most able or knowledgeable) individuals.

Perhaps of even greater significance was the fact that younger groups, by utilizing the abilities of their most knowledgeable individuals, were even more likely to show superior *average member performance.* That is, group scores of younger groups most often outranked the average of the individual scores in their own group *and* the score of the *best* individual in the group. Therefore, relying on one "expert" does not always produce the best score, while relying on the group most often will. In short, younger groups tended to more effectively discover and use their people resources.

One factor seemed to be their flexibility in shifting leadership on each decision to a member who seemed best able to handle that item. In groups composed of older men, it appeared that the individual members were more interested in preserving status, exercising (or avoiding) leadership, and avoiding looking bad to their peers. Consequently, some such individuals tended not to contribute as much to group discussion.

Many studies support the notion that group trust and familiarity with group problem-solving processes are critical in determining group effectiveness. Some researchers suggest that the "habits of managerial office" may have undermined older groups' performance. This tendency of some older managers to dictate decisions may be an age-related cultural phenomenon and the result of "learned expectations" that decisions are best made alone. Much empirical research indicates that the tendency of older individuals to rely on one expert may not be as useful as it was once perceived to be. Others also suggest that younger people may have far more experience (beginning with their academic studies) in group process work and group decision making than many older people do. They may be less concerned with status and control, less competitive in a group setting, and more able to focus on achieving optimum results than some older individuals.

The foregoing discussion clearly indicates that where older employees are expected to increasingly operate in, and contribute to, group activities, they may need to be trained or counseled in how to become more effective group contributors. Since the differences in group performance may seem to be generational—that is, attributable to the way each person was raised, educated, and socialized in the workplace—there should be no inherent reason that some of these habits cannot be overcome. While some individuals may be resistant, most people of any age can, and will, change their behavior if they find it desirable or advantageous to do so. Similarly, interviews and follow-up discussions we have conducted with 242 older (over 55 years old) first-line supervisors and midlevel managers (divided about equally between government and private industry) concerning obstacles to developing teamwork have indicated the following facts about many older managers:

- About a third of them were not used to working in teams except in competitive situations.

- Many of them believed that informal teams were often cliques and were to be avoided.

- Generally, they saw work on the job as usually organized for individual contribution so that group activity was not possible or at least was discouraged.

- They did not know very much about working cooperatively—the meaning of cooperation was seen largely as not making waves, not getting in someone else's way, and giving help only when it was asked for.

- They saw "a team player" as one who goes along with the coach (decision maker), does not dissent, and plays his or her assigned role.

- They viewed volunteering help as taboo, an insult, or something to be treated with suspicion.

- They had often been raised under the autocratic model of management and saw asking for, or accepting, help as a sign of weakness or dependency.

- They were in the habit of relying on "experts," which tended to make them passive in the presence of such people.

- They tended to see teamwork as an agreement that a problem was solved, regardless of the methods used ("going along to get along" was considered acceptable behavior). Even when intellectually committed to teamwork, they lacked the skills to make it work.

A few of these older participants went so far as to suggest that they might be socially out-of-date and need training in how to work more cooperatively in groups. Some suggested that perhaps the reason for quality circles and other short-lived cooperative "fads" was this same difficulty in being able to cooperate. These older people often said that they (and other older employees who worked for them) had much to contribute to group problem solving but frequently did not feel comfortable doing so.

ADDITIONAL SOURCES OF WORK-GROUP CONFLICT

The literature on older workers cites several other sources of work-group conflict that may affect older employees' participation and therefore should be of concern to supervisors and managers as well as the workers themselves.

Generational Conflicts

A few decades ago, it was common to hear talk about a "generation gap" in values. However, research about that time supported the conclusion that many features of the generation gap were contrived rather than real. Perhaps this is why we hear so much less about that notion today. But there is still a problem here. Virtually all age groups tend to believe that the values and even the personalities of other generations are different from their own.

There is some truth to this, and it has led to the new field of study of generational theory.[2] While we have strong reservations about the implications of certain of its findings, we would like to summarize some of its basic assumptions. Generational theory postulates that in today's multigenerational workplace, there is a "clash of generations" between the major components of the present generational culture.

The *silent generation*, born before and during the Great Depression, is supposed to be hardworking and structured, preferring rules, order, and formal hierarchies. The *baby boomers*, the post–World War II generation, is assumed to be interactive and nonauthoritarian, concerned about fairness and workplace participation. The Generation *Xers* grew up during the 1970s and 1980s, the times of the civil rights movement and women's liberation. They are described as self-directed, focused on learning and technology, and computer-oriented. Finally, the Generation Xers are followed by the *millennial* generation, which is seen as confident and flexible but subscribing to stricter ethics and a holistic philosophy.

While we don't doubt that considerable differences exist between the members of these generations, the same is true for any team, group, or committee—age diversity requires a closer look at each individual and his or her talents, experience, and expertise. Any generational stereotyping may be rather counterproductive in trying to analyze multigenerational groups and their performance.

Supervisors encounter the generation gap most commonly when a person makes negative generalizations about another person on the basis of assumptions about the values of the other person's age group. These generalizations can usually be detected by the use of absolutes, stated or implied, such as "all you kids think of . . ." or "all you old folks act like . . ." or the use of certain derogatory terms. For the benefit of maintaining good group operating processes, such "put-downs" should be confronted effectively and not allowed to pass even if they are used in a genuinely humorous sense.

Resentment of Seniority

Older workers are the most likely to be advantaged by seniority rules and agreements. Employees of organizations where seniority counts for job security usually buy into the system to the degree to which they gain seniority with the passing years. Therefore, resentment over seniority is not likely to be overt, but when there is a threat of layoffs or an economic downturn, it is not uncommon for spontaneous bickering, indirect negative behaviors, or snide remarks to unsettle an organization or group as tensions mount.

Blocking Advancement of Younger Employees

As the baby-boom bubble arrives at the older end of the life scale and older employees can stay longer on the job, some people expect that generational strife may increase. Though such a sentiment may be observable only occasionally, an increasing number of younger people may be wishing that older employees would move out of the workforce and give them a chance. This problem most often flares when a younger person believes that the "old-timers" are holding jobs that they do not need. A supervisor might confront this attitude, which is often based on the assumption that the only needs for work are economic, by discussing among employees what work means to different people and why a person may want to hold on to a job long after his or her basic needs for sustenance could be met by their retirement program.

Competition from Women and Minorities

There is occasional mention in management literature of resentment toward older employees by other protected classes of employees, such as (presumably younger) women and minorities. Since ADEA legislation was passed, some older employees have been placed in direct competition with some other people covered by affirmative action plans when personnel actions are contemplated. Since some older employees also fall into one or more of these other categories as well, the situation can become very complicated. Supervisors should be alert to this type of potential conflict and possibly seek expert counsel if such problems arise. If there is a union, its position may also have to be taken into consideration. Where older employees seem to gain or lose relative to other groups, reactions on both sides of the equation may have to be explored.

The Illness and Handicap Conflict

Although employers would have a difficult time preventing employees who have recovered from illness or injury or who would now be labeled handicapped from returning to work, some studies indicate that other employees sometimes cause trouble for them. A study sponsored by the American Cancer Society found that fully recovered employees returning to their former jobs sometimes faced hostility, usually expressed by sarcastic remarks, shunning, and changes in assignments.

They even found that, despite the law, 13% were denied reemployment because of their cancer history, and 35% perceived some form of discrimination after returning to work. Studies have also shown that a significant percent of stroke victims who are later capable of full employment report resentment by supervisors and coworkers when they are able to return to the job. There seems at times to be almost a sense of embarrassment or resentment toward people who return to the workplace after a serious ailment.

Therefore, despite the legal rights of elderly people, who are subject to some of these illnesses in greater proportion than other segments of the workforce, supervisors and managers do not appear always to be doing a good job in defusing conflicts arising from such illnesses. All of this indicates a deep need for conflict-resolution skills by supervisors and managers as well as an exceptional sensitivity to potential, age-related conflicts. These differences are particularly important where employees are expected to work as a self-managed team.

OLDER EMPLOYEES' CONTRIBUTIONS TO WORK-GROUP SUCCESS

On the positive side of the ledger, examples are growing of organizations, teams, and work groups that combine the efforts of young and old for their mutual benefit. One authority cites an example of a food industry corporation with a mandatory retirement age of 55 that, after having restricted the hiring of new production and marketing personnel for 13 years, discovered that the average age of its employees was nearing 50 and decided to extend the retirement age.[3] However, the company's union opposed the notion that older workers should be separated or given special treatment. They argued that all employees can work in unison, with everyone enthusiastic about his or her work.

The company consequently adopted a personnel management policy that encouraged older workers to fend off the feeling that they were too old to work or that they should resign or retire. Coworkers and colleagues were expected to provide emotional and other types of personal support to older employees. As a result, the company reported that older employee morale had risen noticeably and that the overall atmosphere was more vigorous even among younger employees.

Examples of youth-age cooperation in other industrial nations with rapidly rising older populations are also becoming more common. Several studies suggest that companies should attempt to ensure that enclaves of older employees do not develop unless there is a very special reason for their existence. One study argues that, while there may be much perceived security and mutual support within such an enclave, much of this support may be directed to setting unsatisfactory work standards and resisting change. In addition, the enclave group's relations with other departments or work groups can become strained. Thus, many experts stress the benefits of a balanced age structure within the organization and within its components.

Information on decision making by younger and older individuals indicates ways that the strengths of each may be used to complement those of the other to produce superior results. We have found that, often, younger managers are more willing to shift authority within the group, to listen to, and accept, the special expertise of another person, and to be flexible and tolerant of others. However, they also tend to more readily discount unpopular viewpoints and the inherent risks in a situation. Their self-confidence tends to lead them to overrate their abilities, and they have some tendency to be intolerant of details in an unfamiliar field. By contrast, older managers seem better able to appraise the value of new information and tend to minimize risk by seeking more reliable direction from authority figures and expert opinion. These, of course, are general opinions and may not hold up in a given situation.

Given these types of findings, many researchers suggest that a balanced team of older and younger managers or professionals who respect the abilities and contribution of the other group members and who are sophisticated in the ways of team information processing, conflict resolution, and nonthreatening confrontation skills can produce superior results. The techniques of interpersonal problem solving that are available to the group and its members as well as the maturity of group members seem to be critical factors in group effectiveness.

Almost all organizational units possess at least two, often less recognized identities. The most obvious is that of the *formal* organization, exemplified by the organizational chart, composed of the supervisor, line producers, and support staff. In this structure, the supervisor acts as leader and most often interacts with each subordinate on a one-to-one basis, though sometimes organizing and directing team efforts. The *informal* organization is based on the often powerful and varied relationships among the team members themselves. The informal groups that arise from these relationships may be even more powerful than the formal structure. Such a group may have its own informal leaders to whom the members are more committed than they are to their formal supervisor. It may even be able to pull down the appointed supervisor through misdirection of action, formation of a union, or sabotage. Or it may support the supervisor and contribute greatly to that person's success.

Informal groups start by providing social interaction and support for each other. They teach newcomers the ropes (though not always what the supervisor would desire), provide comfort and often protection for each other, and may contribute greatly to an individual member's success or failure. These groups often link the group members to the grapevine and to other sources of knowledge and help throughout the organization. Informal groups are usually loosely formed, and a given employee may actually be part of several of them—such as an informal information network in a car pool, a social group that regularly plays cards together at lunchtime, a women's network group, and the company bowling league. For some employees, membership in these informal groups makes their job enjoyable. The informal group often has an important influence on whether a person retires or continues to work, both through its attitude about the alternatives and by the way that it communicates group values to its members. It can also make the job a home away from home or a living hell for an individual. Informal group members often provide the caring, pleasurable support system that a retiree misses after leaving the workplace.

Informal groups arise naturally in any social setting. Such groups and their leaders often determine how much the work group produces. Despite the supervisory ego involved in the statement, "A supervisor makes things happen," the supervisor may produce mediocre results if the work group decides that is what *it* wants. The protective conspiracy of "let's not do too much or they'll be expecting it all the time" characterizes the training of new employees in many organizations. Employee skills of foot-dragging, goldbricking, sabotage, blowing the whistle on the boss, and staging accidents are well documented. Here the issue is that strong, informal work groups often determine relationships, group norms, standards of behavior, and even output, in a very real sense.

The wise supervisor works with the informal group if possible, rather than against it. While the informal group greatly influences the social system and even solves its own "family problems," the knowing supervisor can do much to help this type of organization work toward mutually beneficial ends. The wise supervisor creates innovative policies and methods within his or her sphere of authority that foster cooperative efforts (especially at the worker level, where there is more likely to be antiorganizational bias). Older employees often have inordinate influence in the informal group. However, if excluded from it, they are likely to leave the organization.

TRAINING FOR INTERGENERATIONAL COOPERATION

Workshops that confront the stereotypes about aging and provide reality data about the physical, intellectual, and emotional aspects of the aging process are becoming increasingly common. Most often offered to supervisors and managers, these training programs aim at enhancing each participant's ability to maximize the contribution of each older employee. Victoria Kaminski has described such programs offered at the Lawrence Livermore National Laboratory, which train all the supervisors from one division or department at one time. "Since these supervisors create the organizational climate for their workers, it is helpful for them all to be dealing from the same information base."[4]

Such training has often been justified by a set of assumptions that recognize that some older people do function or behave differently in many instances. When younger (not necessarily young) employees are ignorant of the realities of these differences (which may not be negative) and consequently believe the myths about older people, hold prejudices, or make unwarranted assumptions, it is likely to show in their words and actions. This can obviously hurt morale, produce conflict, and lessen team effectiveness.

It has been suggested, therefore, that supervisory personnel should be given training that explains the peculiarities and realities of both older and younger employees as well. This thought has been rejected by some, on the basis that all supervisors have at least experienced youth, whereas not all of them have as yet been old. However, such arguments miss the point that is relevant here. Companies can easily devise team-building training that includes the following:

- Information on the myths and realities about all age groups as they are related to group activities, problem solving, and decision making
- Information, exercises, or case studies on ways to resolve conflicts related to age differences
- Activities and exercises that make it easy for participants to try out new behaviors and attitudes related to age issues in an accepting and emotionally safe environment
- Team-building activities where the special contribution of each person is recognized and maximized and age differentials are discussed to see whether there are lingering problems
- The latest skill-building techniques for nonthreatening confrontation, ways to improve team communication, and ways to improve group problem-solving skills
- A focus on maximizing team productivity, gaining harmony, recognizing individual contribution, enhancing cooperation, and building team spirit
- Provision for follow-up and individual counseling for individuals who appear to have a special problem when dealing with people of other ages or who find some types of cooperation difficult

The last item may seem strange to some readers, but some individuals do have trouble freeing themselves from age stereotypes and adopting behaviors that encourage interactions with people of different age groups. Some of these individuals might benefit from being able to talk out their problems with an effective counselor.

In most cases, if older workers are to become an effective part of work teams, it is necessary for the groups to engage in "skull practices," as do football teams, to talk over plans and strategies, review past actions, learn new methods, or consciously build team spirit and effectiveness. This frequent processing of team behavior in a healthy, positive fashion is essential to productive team development and high performance that allow employees of all ages to meet their needs for personal and group accomplishment.

CHAPTER 12

Overcoming Low Individual and Work Group Productivity

Low productivity of individuals or of whole work groups, regardless of their age, may have quite different causes. In the case of older employees, however, those causes are generally rather specific, and, once they are diagnosed and remedied, productivity should rise again to satisfactory levels.

In the earlier chapter on motivation and morale, we determined that past discriminatory practices and wrongful procedures are often to blame for the lack of motivation and productivity of older workers. Many organizations continue, sometimes unintentionally, in their routine of not offering older workers their due share of challenging assignments and of chances for advancement as well as opportunities for learning new skills and for personal growth.

In other instances, we have witnessed certain individuals or whole groups of workers being affected by the experience of cultural conflict and maladjustment, caused by changes in management, merger situations, or market conditions. The outcome of being exposed to a failed organizational culture may be job withdrawal or "retirement on the job" by individuals or whole groups. Through job withdrawal, a person transfers and displaces his or her creativity, social cleverness, and interest from the organization to the pursuit of personal objectives while remaining employed. This is practiced in a way that enhances life on the job for the individual but at a great loss for the organization so affected. It's a payback for poor management and a defunct culture.

Therefore, if low output occurs, it is the responsibility of supervisors and managers to detect the motivational or other causes and assist the employees to overcome them. In particular, older workers, who spent a lifetime developing their knowledge, skills, and abilities and adding to their experience, are such an important and indispensable resource for organizations that it needs to be nourished and supported rather than being squandered.

The research on aging reinforces this more positive view of older employees, and many of our observations in this book corroborate these findings. For example, we have noted the following:

- Age-related changes in physical ability, cognitive performance, and personality have little effect on older workers' productivity except in the most physically demanding tasks.
- Creativity and intellectual capability do not necessarily decline with age. For instance, the artistic ability of musicians in general rises with age and does not decline until very late in their lives.
- The work ethics are much stronger among older workers than among their younger peers. This is also reflected in generally lower absenteeism and less turnover for older employees.
- With suitable methods, older people can be trained or retrained as effectively as anyone. Informational abilities and good judgment either rise or are at least maintained in later age in the majority of people.
- Older workers tend to be more satisfied with their general job situation. Also, if treated without bias, they show greater perception, insight, and patience than their younger peers and often come up with workable solutions to problems.

This list is not intended to repeat and rehash older people's virtues but is a reminder to take the older person seriously whenever performance problems develop. A decline in older employees' performance should be considered as unusual, requiring a serious effort in finding the cause and proper remedy.

RESPONSES TO DISCRIMINATION

If older employees sense supervisory avoidance or discrimination, they have a limited number of ways to respond and to deal with their frustration. The most common coping devices include *giving up and withdrawing from the job* (but remaining employed), *leaving* (which could mean resigning or transferring to another position), and *getting angry and getting even* (which includes both passive behaviors and open confrontation). Of course, the proper response of the supervisor would be mutual problem solving, but that approach still seems rarely used when an older employee is involved. There may be other responses, but the ones mentioned show some interesting variations with important practical applicability.

Giving up and Withdrawing from the Job

As mentioned before, this response does not always lead to unsatisfactory performance, but a price is always paid. It's what we call working by the book," leading to diminished collaboration and behavioral negation at work. For lack of a better term, Mohrman has named this type of behavioral job withdrawal *disempowerment*, where people are prevented from "being able to make a difference in the attainment of individual, group and organizational goals."[1] Looking at it from a different angle, it is self-protective behavior of people who try to come to terms with their lack of control and participation in the workplace. They feel helpless, often angry, and react by performing their duties in a minimal way.

Leaving

If an employee resigns to join another firm, accepts an early retirement option, or agrees to a transfer to another assignment or location, often involving lower pay or less responsibility, the problem seems to be solved to everybody's satisfaction. However, in reality it's not. The organization loses the skills, experience, and special knowledge of a longtime employee. Certain proprietary know-how may migrate to a

competitor or be no longer available. The transfer, in particular including a downgrade in conditions, may just be a temporary solution
to a continuing problem. The evidence suggests that, while a voluntary
migration may seem to resolve the issue, it represents a supervisory
failure, which ought to be avoided with proper cooperation between
employee and management to the benefit of the organization.

Getting Angry and Getting Even

To compensate for their frustrations in a failed job situation, people
may take different avenues to come to terms with it. The majority resort to a reactive job withdrawal, which allows them to stay employed
but with minimal effort and engagement. Others draw particular motivation from actively renouncing any interest in the job, thus obtaining
a renewed sense of control over their work situation. The angry person
may well "go underground" and wage a passive form of guerrilla warfare against the offending supervisor or organization. When people are
tenured or protected by a union contract, they may feel secure enough
to let their anger and frustration manifest themselves in some overt
action, confronting their supervisor or filing grievances—waging a
no-win battle that is unproductive and costly in time, energy, and resources. Such conflicts may benefit from mediation or basic conflict-
resolution skills, which may need to be taught to a greater spectrum of
people in organizations.

RESOLVING PRODUCTIVITY PROBLEMS
ON A MUTUAL BASIS

Many older employees feel trapped by their many years of service
and the concurrent pension entitlements and, on the other hand, certain family responsibilities. They may be looking for advancement that
they realize is unlikely to be achieved. Prospects for the promotion of
older employees hardly seem rosy. Advancement, however, is not the
only way to increase job satisfaction. As we have learned in earlier

chapters of this book, older workers enjoy the mental and psychological stimulation of the workplace and being part of a close-knit team. Recognition of a person's contribution and expertise as well as a new and challenging assignment go a long way in restoring motivation and unleashing unexpected productivity. Giving attention to these factors is an important responsibility of supervision. Below, we discuss some ways that supervisors and management have taken to gain a positive resolution of productivity problems.

Effective Confrontation

When people are not pulling their weight, it does not always mean that they are unable to. However, to turn them around may take a carefully structured confrontation. Performance problems should be stated clearly and factually, but in an unemotional and neutral way. The consequence of the person's behavior on the job and the effects on the team or the organization should be stated without threat or evaluation, and the degree of seriousness of the problem should be communicated appropriately. All in all, it's important that the supervisor confront, rather than avoid, the issue or seek an easy out. Older employees with symptoms of job withdrawal tend to consume management time and organizational resources in the long run. Therefore, supervisors should not sidetrack the problem (e.g., by transferring the person) but use the method of effective confrontation.

Effective Counseling

The anger, despair, or self-deception that leads to job withdrawal behaviors is not healthy. It is stressful and may easily lead to low self-esteem, unhappiness, and even illness. People with such problems should be offered help in getting on with their lives. In some cases, this type of help can be provided by the supervisor or others who are trained or experienced in effective listening and counseling skills. Where the problem is deeper, professional counseling may be a good investment.

Problem Solving

Once the problem has been clarified, it is important to allow the employee time to respond fully, stating his or her own case, and for the counselor (especially if it is the supervisor or manager) to listen carefully to what the employee is saying. Argument at this point is futile. Each person's view is valid to him or her, and only by accepting each other's views as such can we progress to solving the problem. If a disagreement develops, determining who is right and who is wrong may not be very useful for changing behavior. An active, two-way discussion of the problem and how to resolve it is critical. Both parties should search for new ways to cooperate if the issue is to be dealt with effectively.

Supervisory Support

The supervisor, who can get beyond past failures and mistakes, may be in a position to help employees to reevaluate their situation, setting clear, new goals and developing a specific plan for changes in productivity. This leads to a sense of a mutual win-win relationship between the two parties. While in some organizations there still is a strong tradition of top-down management and one-sided operational decisions, the notion of a truly cooperative, mutual problem-solving approach between employee and supervisor, with both parties fully involved, seems to be the only sound basis for overcoming productivity problems.

Putting Some Fun into the Workplace

In general, people don't think of work in terms of fun. There may be things that, in effect, are fun, like getting some positive results, enjoying the camaraderie of a good team, or being a mentor to a coworker. From the viewpoint of the supervisor, however, letting people have fun at work is not about Friday beer busts or employee appreciation parties, but it means recognizing them as human beings with all their dreams and aspirations. Employees, in particular, older workers, want to be treated as mature and responsible adults, able to use their creative abilities and talents, with the opportunity to live out their own personal values. It's fun because people are fully engaged, have total responsibility for work-related decisions, and are accountable for results. Obviously, it's difficult to give up conventional "management" and the desire to control others. But the results can be astounding when changing a stale and inefficient work environment to a place of unusual motivation and productivity.

INDIVIDUAL RESPONSIBILITY

As older employees arrive at the later working period of their lives, they must understand that there are different choices for them to pursue and that it is their individual responsibility if and how they ensure continued employment.

First, there is always the option of early retirement, which is personally riskier and more unpredictable than most people realize. It may involve possible idleness, social life changes, and loss of skills and meaningful work. It also tends to be a one-way street if people can't stand the inactivity. It takes creativity and much personal discipline to build new activities or another career to fill the void that has been created.

As a second alternative, people prefer to stay employed, but they feel they have put in their time, have worked hard in the past, and with that earned the right to take it easier and enjoy the final years while collecting their full paycheck. Others, faced with the possibility of corporate restructuring and downsizing, expect to survive, hunker down, and hope no one will notice them. In both of these scenarios, people face the risk of elimination of their jobs, because in reality their work and contribution to the organization may not be productive enough to guarantee continued employment.

In these situations, people seem to be trapped in a stressful and debilitating cycle that is not useful and productive for either the individual or the organization. They might well devote considerable thought and energy to how to break out of this self-defeating behavior. One of the immediate benefits is a more positive mind-set and attitude that comes from being productive and full of energy. While the supervisor may not see and acknowledge the particular effort, our sense of achievement helps rebuild our inner pride and self-esteem, making us healthier persons.

In a recent article entitled "Job Satisfaction Starts with Enthusiastic Attitude," Billy Arcement offers certain tips on how to make one's job a more satisfying experience and remove stress, unhappiness, and frustration from the environment.[2] They are as follows:

- *Take pride in your work.* Give every action the best you have to offer. Once you have done your best, you can be proud.

- *Bring enthusiasm to your work.* No matter how boring your job is, try to be enthusiastic about it. By being enthusiastic, you begin to view your job differently. Don't dismiss this idea before trying it first.

- *Be creative.* Look beyond the routine parts of your job and see if you can come up with ways to make your work more fun, exciting, and rewarding.

- *Become the expert.* Try to study the field your job is in for one hour a day. Concentrate on details, take notes, and become an expert in that discipline, which opens up opportunities for advancement. It also builds enthusiasm.

- *Be professional and cooperative.* Always work at the highest standard and try to be available to those who need your expertise. Professionals enjoy their work and are respected by their peers.

By implementing these ideas, Arcement feels we can make our own pastures greener and don't feel the need to look toward distant places for better job satisfaction.

THE ROAD TO CONSTRUCTIVE CHANGE

When an older employee who has been around for a while performs inadequately, ask why. Do not accept the notion that such employees are "at the top of their grade" or that "they can't be motivated." Virtually all employees want to enjoy their jobs as much as possible. Help them to get on with it. When we begin to act as though we really believe the following six points, low productivity, especially of older workers, may cease to be a problem.

1. Expending physical and mental effort in useful work (on or off the job) is as natural as play or rest.
2. People exercise self-direction or self-control in working toward objectives to which they are committed.
3. When rewards, in particular nonmonetary ones—good feelings, recognition, a sense of achievement, job satisfaction, and so on— are closely related to achieving certain goals, they build commitment to these goals.
4. When conditions are supportive and rewarding, the average person is ready to accept and even seek responsibility.
5. Most people in any organization can contribute creative and innovative ideas to improving organizational operations and solving problems.
6. In most organizations, the intellectual potential of the average employee is only partly used.

This modern restating of Douglas McGregor's "Theory Y" assumptions about human nature and behavior is applicable to our whole working population, but in particular to older workers, who can add considerable experience, knowledge, and know-how to the equation.[3]

Some important issues to consider:

- The lack of motivation and productive energy often is a response to frustrations at work. "Withdrawing from the job" may even be self-protective behavior of people trying to come to terms with their lack of control at their job. Have you ever observed coworkers in your organization openly scorning their supervisor's directions to compensate for their frustrations on the job?
- "Job satisfaction starts with an enthusiastic attitude," writes Billy Arcement. Do you agree? Are you proud about what you

do, are you trying to learn more about your job, and are you supporting your work environment with cooperative behavior and a positive attitude?

- Is your organization's culture helping your job satisfaction by giving you the opportunity to make work-related decisions, by allowing you to be creative and make use of your intellectual abilities, and by providing you with recognition and a sense of achievement?

CHAPTER 13

Creating Alternative Work Programs and Flexible Benefits for Older Employees

While it appears that many employers are indifferent to the needs of older people for at least part-time work, a rapidly growing number of organizations are not. The following well-documented examples of what creative people, organizations, and companies are doing to encourage older people to keep producing are drawn from dozens of sources and represent some of the best efforts that others can emulate. Also, while fewer organizations lack any type of retirement transition program, a growing number of innovative programs around the country offer useful and productive models. A few examples of these are described below.

Certain organizations, for example, offer a retirement transition program that permits employees 55 and older to work 20–32 hours a week for as long as they and their employer wish. Such employees often get proportional benefits, partial to full medical insurance, proportional vacation, sick leave, and even in some cases stock options and profit sharing. Employees already retired can sometimes resume work through the program. Such "senior associates," as they are sometimes called, often serve as mentors, troubleshooters, and backup in managerial and technical fields. At times, senior associates also receive extra pay, and many are reluctant to part with these benefits to fully retire.

Builders Emporium, a chain of California-based retail home centers, has redesigned many of its jobs to "accommodate older workers" and "encourage their continued loyalty and presence." In doing so, they recast the job of store clerk, which constituted about two-thirds of their total jobs. They virtually eliminated heavy lifting by clerks by assigning night crews of younger workers to restock the shelves and emphasized salesmanship for those employees who attended the public. As a rule, the older staff workers knew the merchandise better and were more people-focused. By redesigning these jobs, sales personnel fatigue lessened, and the turnover rate dropped substantially.

Wells Fargo has come up with imaginative programs to forestall burnout. A sabbatical program called "personal growth leave" allows "employees with ten or more years of service . . . to take up to three months fully paid leave to pursue a project of their choice."

Mitre Corporation, a high-end technology firm employing over 5,000 people, encourages its older employees to stay in the workforce through phased retirement, part-time assignments, and sabbaticals and through their innovative "Reserves at the Ready" program. This program gives employees with at least ten years of service the option to become part-time, on-call workers on special projects throughout the company. Older workers also mentor their younger peers and share their expertise and insider knowledge of the agencies Mitre serves. The "reserves" include employees experienced in technical, administrative, and secretarial jobs. Mitre's director of quality of work life said the company benefits from these programs, especially since "the average age of its employees is about 45 years—significantly higher than the national average."

But innovative, flexible retirement options are not solely the province of companies. Sarah Fister Gale, a writer for Workforce Management, offers an intriguing case of phased retirement from the academic world.[1] Appalachian State University, which belongs to the University of North Carolina system, allows faculty members over age 50 to work half-time at half their salary for up to three years while collecting partial pension benefits. A retired English professor commented that the half-time salary with the pension and a drop to a lower tax bracket actually increased his monthly income. It enabled him to teach every day while being exempted from committees and university politics. "It was an almost perfect life," he said. "I regret that I couldn't do it for a few more years."

Ultratech, Inc., a maker of photolithography systems in San Jose, California, was one of the few companies in Silicon Valley to offer phased retirement. Ultratech didn't have the youthful workforce of other high-tech competitors—many of the employees had been with the company for more than 20 years. The reason for introducing the plan was to stem the loss of older employees with critical expertise and knowledge. Employees as young as 50 years got the option to reduce their schedules or work on a contract basis. "Phased retirement forces managers to create a transition plan for retirees," Heidi Ordwein, director of human resources, explained, "and to think about mentoring of a replacement." It helps retirees to remain active and stay connected. "We want our people to know we still value them," she said.[2]

To strengthen job security for their older employees, many companies are engaged in new career training. McDonald's Corporation created its McMasters Program to train and place people over age 55. Sterile Design "uses minishifts to accommodate those interested in working less than full time." At another versatile employer of older workers, "flexible work alternatives, which have encouraged a high percentage of people over 65 to stay on the job, include rehearsal retirement, tapering off, temporary or permanent part time work, job sharing, flex time, consulting contracts and a retiree pool for work during peak periods." Aerospace Corporation of southern California saw the loss of highly skilled employees to retirement as a competitive disadvantage, so it launched a program called "casual employment." Under this program, an employee can work 1,000 hours a year (approximately half-time) without his or her pension benefits being affected. Such companies want to keep producers.

None of these programs are aimed at favoring older workers over younger ones; rather, they represent a coming to grips with workforce realities. The retiree job banks established by such socially responsible firms as Travelers Insurance, Wells Fargo Bank, Combustion Engineering, and Grumman Corporation provide part-time or full-time work in their own facilities as well as referring retirees to other firms in their area that are seeking older workers.

Even temporary-help agencies are looking hard for older people. At Manpower, Inc., the largest temporary agency in the world, senior workers constitute more than 25% of the worldwide workforce. Manpower contracts with clients for both short- and long-term (up to several years) assignments for its older employees. MS International, a large personnel services firm, estimates that 15% of the company's temporary employees are over 60 years of age.

Daniel Knowles, a pioneer in advancing ideas for continued employment of older workers, a former vice president for human resources at Grumman Corporation, and a board member of the National Council on Aging, once said that "most companies treat older workers with benign neglect. There is a type of discrimination going on that's very, very subtle. In fact, those who discriminate usually aren't aware they are doing it. Ironically, they are generally middle-aged themselves." Knowles contended that it was up to the private sector to take creative and positive steps to encourage new or continuing employment for older workers. Grumman, for instance, established a "temporary/part time/on call" pool of Grumman retirees when a survey revealed that 50% of its retirees would like such a pool. This, Knowles claimed, "is partly in response to the continuing respect . . . employees know the company has for its older staffers." Further, Knowles claimed, "we show in dozens of ways that we value our senior employees." This positive note contrasts sharply with the "benign neglect" that Knowles referred to earlier. Grumman's job bank, incidentally, filled over 50% of the company's temporary employment needs.

Whether we are retirees ourselves, people with a vested interest in the soundness of the Social Security system, or young people paying taxes, each of us has an investment in finding ways to ensure that older employees can continue to work if they wish to.

SOURCES OF HELP

The American Association of Retired Persons (AARP), knowing that many people prefer continued work to retirement, offers a workbook for conducting preretirement seminars, which includes a section on work alternatives and focuses on why people work and the advantages of doing so. It encourages companies to bring employees into "life-planning" programs as early as possible (often at age 50 or earlier) and offers suggestions on how to reenter the workforce by using self-assessment and a self-directed search method.

AARP maintains a Senior Community Service Employment Program (SCSEP) for unemployed or underemployed workers age 55 and older who are at, or close to, the poverty level. Information can be found at the AARP Web site (www.aarp.com) following directions for the SCSEP program. Similarly, the U.S. Department of Labor offers help with job searches and maintains a listing of job vacancies.

Some companies conduct "working-option sessions" as part of their retirement programs to explain the situation in their own company and how to participate in such work options. Travelers Insurance has long held a special careers session to discuss the organization's "Unretired Program," under which employees who have experienced retirement for six months can come back and, if qualified, fill part-time or full-time jobs—some for a full second career. Walt Disney Company has used a network system to invite retired employees back to work on an as-needed basis. Increasing efforts are being made by more major firms to reverse the early-retirement trend through imaginative part-time and occasional options.

In our age of increasing global trade, examining models from outside the United States may also be fruitful. Helen Ginsburg studied the effects of gradual retirement programs in Sweden and Norway.[3] She found that the partial pension has had a positive effect on its recipients. Partial pensioners value their increased leisure, and many report that they are more rested and energetic. Their health seemed to improve, and absenteeism declined. These factors accounted for the impression among employers that partial pensioners produce more per hour than full-time workers. Such employees were also less likely than full-time workers of the same age to become disabled or unemployed, and they, in effect, contributed to the national wealth.

WIN-WIN WORK OPTIONS

In addition to the programs discussed above, some organizations are experimenting with a variety of work arrangements that can meet the needs of employee, supervision, and management at the same time. Researchers are discovering that many people would be quite interested in postretirement work or putting off retirement if they were allowed such options as the following:

- More flexible scheduling (flextime)
- Job sharing
- Part-time employment (usually less than 30 hours per week)
- Consulting
- Seasonal work
- Compressed workweek: 20–30 hours in two to three days
- Short-term projects
- Reduced hours (even with reduced pay)
- Special assignments
- Job rotation—flexible shifts
- A chance to do company work at home (a high-tech type of cottage industry)
- Contracted work
- A resource person for self-managed teams

Sweden's experience with the partial pension plan demonstrates that reductions in hours can be implemented in a wider variety of ways and in more occupations than conventional wisdom suggests, especially when management is cooperative. Ken Dychtwald and Joe Flower, recognized authorities on aging workers, report that "as people grow older they might want to work less or less frequently rather than to stop working. They often don't want to work as often or perhaps as hard. Some people believe that the lines between the working and non-working will blur."[4] Major companies now have retiree-relations directors, and many others are beginning to place older workers' expertise within their human resources departments.

At-home work or projects that allow a person's expertise to be used only on an as-needed basis can create substantial cost savings to the organization. Many of these new forms of work arrangements can reduce on-the-job idleness by using people's services only when required, rather than having them on the payroll or laying them off when work is slow. Not incurring the fringe benefits and other overhead costs involved when people are not full-time employees sometimes makes it possible for the organization to pay the part-time employee higher rates. With many of these working arrangements, it is also sometimes easier to judge the value of the work performed rather than assume that the real value is a function of the number of hours invested.

Flexible work policies tend to pay off by allowing people to continue and willingly contribute to our national wealth, to the organization, and to their own income, health, and sense of well-being. Employers who maintain options for their employees to continue working obviously gain from the process; the others have only their fears, questionable assumptions, and indifference to deal with.

A classic survey by Catalyst, a research group promoting women's issues in business, found that for 70% of the managers interviewed, retention of an experienced employee was the primary reason for offering a flexible work schedule in 50 companies studied. Thus, flexible work options tended to be an individual decision rather than a general company policy. About one-third of the companies studied allowed job sharing; those that supported it felt that job sharing retained experienced employees, improved return ratios of people on elder care or maternity leave, and boosted the company's image in the community.

Phased retirement plans, by slowly reducing the number of hours worked each week, allow the employer to retain the services of a valued, trained employee for a longer period of time, while often making the employee's adjustment to retirement less traumatic. Even a onetime reduction to part-time employment permits a compromise between a worker's desire to slow down and the employer's need for his or her skilled and experienced work.

Phased retirement, redesigned jobs to de-emphasize physical tasks or labor, arranged paid sabbaticals, and somewhat liberal job titles for those who voluntarily accept downgrading because of personal infirmities are only a few of the ways in which older employees' productivity is being recaptured. These efforts to stabilize an organization's workforce help reduce turnover, save on training costs, and ensure continuity of policies for those organizations wise enough to conserve their older employee resources.

Job sharing, telecommuting, and longer, but fewer, days per week are very viable options for resolving employee shortages if they are done right. For instance, jobs that are boring, tedious, and stressful, physically or mentally, are usually very suitable for job sharing. Job sharing is a viable option when a full-time opening cannot be filled because the skills needed are in short supply or there is a general labor shortage and when employees (or applicants) need to do something else for part of the time, such as attend college or care for children or older relatives. Also, this approach often works when an employer wants to avoid layoffs during an economic downturn; when a full-time employee needs or wants to reduce work hours and is willing to split his or her job with someone else; or when a company is growing, and new jobs are being created. Many organizations fill a slot with a full-time person when only a part-time person is needed, and Parkinson's Law (that the work tends to expand to fill the time available) takes over—perhaps forever in some cases. A half-time or part-time person may obviate the need for sharing.

The expense and time required to plan and administer a job share arrangement are usually more than compensated for by the gains from the process. These often include:

- retention of talented and experienced older employees who otherwise might leave
- options for coverage—when one person is ill or absent, the other can often fill in for him or her
- reduced absenteeism when one "partner" is faced with a family or other crisis
- increased quality (where the job is boring and/or fatiguing, errors may decline)
- greater productivity

A shared job, for example, may double the ideas, creativity, and energy that go into it.

Travelers Insurance, for instance, has largely gained such benefits, as each week several hundred retirees work throughout the company in professional, clerical, and secretarial positions. Ranging in age from the late 50s to the mid-80s, they also fill in during peak work times or when other employees are absent or on vacation. An older employee who decides against retirement is immediately available and able to contribute to the organization at once, without the need to learn anything about the organization's culture, rules and regulations, policies and procedures, or traditions and work ethics. An older employee knows the job to be done and does it. Contrast this with hiring a new person for the job if the older person had opted for retirement.

Many employee-benefit experts believe that flexible work arrangements produce a competitive advantage, particularly when such policies are formal, widely supported by management, and closely monitored. Tracking and encouraging such practices throughout the organization seem critical. Aetna, for example, instituted programs to offer part-time work, job sharing, at-home work, flexible schedules, family leaves (which include up to six months of unpaid leave for family emergencies), and referral services to locate help for care of elderly relatives or children. This has been a successful part of a wider program to recruit and retain the best people available. When properly managed, such programs definitely have a payback many times over for the time and resources expended. Such enlightened management is bound to improve America's competitive advantage.

CONCLUSION: KEEPING PACE WITH CHANGES IN THE WORKFORCE

In the preceding chapters, we looked at older workers from different vantage points:

- In Part I, we took the angle of society facing the realities of an aging workforce, of their changed inclinations, and of a new and different workplace and exciting organizational cultures. We learned that by 2012 about half of the labor force will be age 48 to 66 and that it is likely to stay active and involved in a different workplace where hierarchies are gone and where it matters to share, to grow, and to feel like family. Yesterday's authoritative manager will change to focus on participation, self-management, and being a role model.

- Part II was dedicated to the role of the older workers, their experience, mature attitude, and renewed motivation—all different from the past. "I think older workers have changed," Jay Kloosterboer, the chief human resource officer of AES Corporation, commented in this context. "They have a different attitude and are now viewed as valuable contributors to the benefit of their organizations."

- In Part III, we covered many of the changes in the organizational environment, which is multigenerational today, needs a different kind of supervisor and manager, thrives on self-managed teams, and has become more sensitive to the problems of age bias and discrimination.

As our journey through the issues of older employees is coming to a close, we would like to focus on seven significant themes, which we believe will stay in the forefront of future developments—many of them interwoven and interrelated—and will increasingly be of importance to society. These seven primary themes are as follows:

1. *The continuing (and even accelerating) medical revolution is generating healthier and longer-living older employees than anticipated.* The statistics on older workers wanting (even demanding) gainful employment may burgeon beyond our wildest dreams. Medical research has succeeded beyond expectations to extend life expectancy and help people to stay physically and mentally more capable than ever before to the very end of their longer lives.

2. *Aging Americans represent an increasingly powerful political lobby, influencing policy making and its impact on business.* Political power will certainly shift more clearly to our older population. Therefore, the necessity of reconciling competing needs of various age and interest groups will intensify. Consequently, greater personal maturity, ethical wisdom, long-term vision, and creative skills will be sorely needed by all of us.

3. *Business competitiveness is increasingly a function of continuous and lifelong learning.* Moving from the Industrial Age into the Information Age has brought about the *knowledge worker*, so crucial to the competitiveness of today's organizations. In addition, the higher level of education of today's workforce creates significant incentives for continued learning, to stay up-to-date and maintain intellectual flexibility.

4. *The need for personal change, flexibility, and self-investment can take each older person to higher levels of success.* The old idea of the way to survive (and possibly succeed) on the job—to hunker down, keep your mouth shut, and do what you are told—has died but is not yet buried in many organizations. At the same time, the organizational ladder is shorter and more crowded as the effects of downsizing and restructuring have set in. For the older person to be successful, this

will mean more self-investment in education and training in a wider range of skills and knowledge and a demand for greater professionalism on the job.

5. *Employing organizations need to create environments and cultures where job satisfaction is higher, so that employees want to stay longer.* For management, this means a change in style and substance. Changes in policies allowing for greater variety in work options and career moves are helpful, but they alone don't do the job. Coming labor shortages will make older employees less dependent on their employers, more demanding of satisfying work and a quality environment, and expecting higher levels of managerial leadership and performance.

6. *Acts of age bias and discrimination are becoming more sensitive and complex, calling for more and more relevant training.* Though age bias and discrimination will still exist, in the future they will be rare rather than common, discouraged rather than tolerated, and made conscious rather than hidden in the minds of the offenders, thereby moderating their effects.

7. *For the health of our society, we must increasingly develop organizational cultures that regard work as healthy, important, and a fun part of our lives.* This will require a major cultural shift away from the negative reservations about work that were cast in the early days of the Industrial Revolution and reinforced by the era of "scientific management." It will also require a new era of exceptional leadership at every level of our organizations and integration of such notions into a comprehensive social philosophy broad enough to crowd out competing visions of work.

If these seven themes prevail, employers may be overwhelmed by an embarrassment of riches in the quality and quantity of our older workforce and a consequent surge in national wealth. The power behind these possibilities is foreshadowed by current research and social developments already under way. Since predicting the future is bound to be imprecise, we will let these themes speak for themselves.

THE MEDICAL REVOLUTION

Current medical research trends could toss all our statistical projections about our older employee workforce into a cocked hat. Without any lengthening of the human life span, we may find that virtually everyone is well and physically and mentally able as long as he or she lives. Here we are not talking about the *average* life expectancy of people (which by the year 2030, without any great changes in medical knowledge or practices, should be about 77 for men and almost 83 for women). Nor are we discussing the limits of human life, which current scientific thinking puts at between 110 and 120 years. As an example of what may happen, we discuss new research in this particular area later in the section.

However, we can infer from the current research that far higher percentages of our population will live out their full span of years and be mentally and physically vigorous to the end of those years. Average life expectancy could get close to the century mark in 20 years if these trends continue. There will be a host of new therapeutic drugs, medical procedures, and devices to contribute to these possibilities. Some of these areas of research and treatment are familiar to most of us, like the "human genome project," mapping the genes of the human body and allowing for elements of gene therapy or at least certain preventive strategies or "personal health plans" to be established for genetically affected individuals in the future.

In addition, there are all kinds of new classes of drugs on the way to bring significant new benefits to the senior population, improving the chances of survival in many types of cancer, cardiovascular illnesses, or Parkinson's disease. Biotechnology and its medical advances are expected to change the practice of health care to a wellness-oriented system that focuses on the majority of the people who are healthy versus the ones who are sick, benefiting patients, doctors, and health insurance alike.

What does all of this mean for older workers and their employers? It means that a lot more people will be a lot older and a lot more able to work to a much later age. This healthier, more able workforce will increasingly demand outlets for its energies, abilities, and talents. The scope of the opportunity for effective use of this human capital is almost beyond belief.

Coming back to the particular issue of life expectancy and certain lines of research in this area, we would like to mention the field of *telomeres*—protein complexes that are found at the end of our chromosomes. It has been found and proven that each time a cell divides—part of the process of regeneration of our body—these telomeres get shorter. With time, this shortening seems to impair the ability of the cell to further divide and reproduce itself. Researchers believe that a better understanding of this telomere shortening process might lead to an ability to influence the process of aging. As a matter of fact, in laboratory tests that add the enzyme telomerase, cells have been seen to reproduce without shortening of telomeres indefinitely.

There is a flip side to this research. In cancer, which is uncontrolled cell growth, telomeres do not shorten when cancer cells divide. In other words, a better understanding of the mechanism of telomere shortening could also be applied to cancer cells and slow their uncontrollable growth.

This is just one example of exciting new research in the area of biotechnology and cell biology. Further information is available at www.infoaging.org, the Web site of the American Federation for Aging Research.

AGING AMERICANS AS A POWERFUL IMPACT ON PUBLIC POLICY

Daily, the political and economic power of older citizens increases, as does their awareness of it. So far, most of this power has been used to redress grievances and achieve fairness for older people. However, some of us worry that this growing clout could be used to gain advantages for seniors at the expense of the needs of other segments of our population. The art of government in a democracy is a public effort to ensure that we govern our society so that *all* its segments are healthy and productive. This cannot be achieved when some are disadvantaged by the unfair gain of others. Consequently, each of us needs to carefully study each policy and law to ensure that it will strengthen all of our society, not just the segments to which we belong.

One such problem of misguided "gerontocracy" is described by Ken Dychtwald in his book *Age Power.* Dychtwald is unhappy with the lobbying power of the American Association of Retired Persons, which today has about 35 million members and generates revenues based on member dues of about $150 million. The AARP's clear focus is to strive for, and defend, higher entitlements—in Social Security, Medicare, or federal taxes—for the elderly, while Dychtwald advocates the need for a new role of the mature segment of the population. This would include embracing needy younger people as mentors, teachers, or foster parents. As community leaders, seniors would have to impart strong values to help interconnect the old and the young. This would help to clear up certain misconceptions of old and young about each other and make the younger generation feel somewhat better about the consequent reduced levels of health care and pension benefits that now seem unavoidable.

There is another side to the problem when we consider the needs of working and nonworking older people. Fully retired people are dependent people—dependent on Social Security, their pension funds, their savings, their investments. Whether we are talking about tax policies, amendments to the Social Security system, or Medicare, public moves to alter the status quo or correct problems can be threatening to people dependent for their living on external forces that are working in society. When we feel so threatened, we are all likely to lash out and support policies that appeal to our need for security (and even our perceived survival needs) without much consideration of their overall long-term effects on others.

Fully retired people tend to find their options narrowing the longer they hold that status. Working people tend to retain the options that they have always had and even gain additional ones as time goes on. They tend to be more in contact with other segments of society, more involved with, and aware of, the needs of other workers because of their daily contacts, and more self-confident because of their daily demonstrated ability to take care of themselves. They may therefore find it easier to develop a measured response to controversial public policies that affect them. The greater the percentage of Americans who are gainfully employed, the more likely that this balanced approach to public policies will occur.

CONTINUOUS AND LIFELONG LEARNING

In a recent report of the Federal Reserve Bank of Cleveland, we read that "the American workforce is becoming increasingly educated as younger generations replace the older ones. Over the past 30 years, the fraction of American workers who did not graduate from high school plummeted from about 36% in 1970 to 10% in 2003. Meanwhile, the share of workers with at least a college degree more than doubled, rising from about 14% to 32%."[1] It's an important development because the higher level of education is a strong incentive to continue on that path. We see similar trends in graduate education, where the part-time and online pursuit of graduate degrees has fueled an ever-growing demand from people who want to continue their education while remaining employed. Nearly 20% of these graduate students get some tuition support from their employers. Online educational courses and programs are the fastest growing segment of higher education in the world.

From the field of psychological theory, we know that self-perception is a powerful factor in enhancing people's motivation to learn. People who see themselves as having greater intellectual abilities pursue "learning goals," reflecting their need for self-enhancement. They develop a certain "mastery orientation" and perceive their intellectual capacity as something they can control and expand.

This, then, translates into the ability to meet ever more difficult challenges by learning and acquiring new skills, leading to healthy personal growth. With time, people choose their level of challenge and develop their personal orientation, but there is no question that successful learning becomes a source of motivation and helps to build self-esteem.

PERSONAL CHANGE, FLEXIBILITY, AND SELF-INVESTMENT

The evolution of workplace changes such as self-directed work groups, boundaryless organizations, and learning organizations can lead to the development of workers who are quite unlike what we have seen in the past. These paeans to ultimate human responsibility, maturity, and self-actualization should sound loud and clear to older employees, especially those who have seen enough of passivity, dependence, and often second-class citizenship in the workplace.

To participate effectively in this new workforce requires training in skills seldom previously offered to older employees, even when they were part of management. These often include rather new interpersonal skills, such as nonthreatening confrontation techniques, conflict-resolution skills, active listening, creative problem-solving methods, cooperative decision making, ways to request help, giving feedback to help others, positive responses to negative situations, dealing with changes, getting your point across, and effectively participating in group meetings. But, as the lines between workers and management blur, most workers are becoming more professional, and management is increasingly dependent on the special know-how and skills of its workers. Consequently, we need workers who are more self-confident, adaptable, and socially competent. At every level, we need leaders who are more visionary, collegial in behavior, and, again, adaptable. This is the new ball game in which older employees will increasingly be playing.

Neither government programs nor employer assistance in updating employee skills and knowledge amounts to much without the dedicated involvement of older employees themselves. We must all develop the habit of self-investment as early in life as we can to ensure that we optimize our mutual future. Our society has a long history of personal passivity, where things were done to us or for us for long periods of our lives without many of us having to make personal decisions to ensure our future. If we simply did our job adequately, things tended to take care of themselves.

Now this is changing. Increasingly, it will be up to each individual to decide how much and what type of ongoing education and developmental activities he or she will engage in. Obsolescence results from a type of mental lethargy that we can no longer afford. In this regard, human involvement in work tends to be total, in the sense that an employee on the job is always involved physically, mentally (cognitively), and interpersonally to some extent.

Unfortunately, it is often the supervisor and the organization that are getting obsolete, rather than the employee. They have failed to see the cognitive (mental) component of the job or undervalued it, thereby wasting potential. If, however, an experienced older machinist were to be transferred to the methods department, made a part of a problem-solving team, or given a special assignment to improve an operation, all of which involve valuing ideas and experience (largely the mental part of the job), intellectual development would be ensured, just as jogging leads to physical strengthening of the body.

Learning on the job and using that learning are a natural need, since our work consumes so much of our time. But learning and application can also be a habit—one that may wither and die if not encouraged. People tend to become obsolescent because they use only a small part of their natural abilities.

EMPLOYEE SATISFACTION AND RETENTION

It seems like a recurrent dilemma: recent surveys predict that as the economy is improving, as many as half of the employees of many organizations will be looking for new jobs.[2] For many employers, these widespread and disrupting defections are disturbing, and they rush to shore up employee support programs with child care, concierge services, and the like to improve retention. Why is it that they fail to understand the roots of these problems?

A recent *Time* magazine article started by saying: "How to make jobs so satisfying that employees want to say . . . *Thank God It's Monday!*" (the title of the article).[3] The article explained that "people who love their jobs feel challenged by their work but in control of it. They have bosses who make them feel appreciated and co-workers they like. They can find meaning in whatever they do." Apparently, that desire for meaning is so strong that sometimes, in particular with unpleasant work, people simply create it. They want to feel engaged, and that satisfaction spills into the rest of their lives.

The article acknowledges the responsibility of supervisors and front-line managers in "joy building" for their workers and makes some recommendations as follows:

1. *Be here now.* Rather then focusing on insincere "employee-appreciation days," the manager should be fully available every day.

2. *Don't be a fair-weather friend.* During tough times, the efforts to en-gage workers should not diminish. These efforts will be remembered once times change again.
3. *See team members as individuals.* Use each employee's strength to get to your goal. If you have a great pitcher, let someone else do the batting.
4. *Remember that silence is not golden.* Don't talk to your employees only when they make a mistake. Recognize their accomplishments.
5. *Let friendship ring.* Having a good friend at work makes an employee happy and productive.
6. *Let the outside world in.* There is nothing wrong with asking your employees about their weekend or about their kids. They become people rather than part of a head count.
7. *Be yourself.* An honest, low-key chat can be just as effective as the celebrity CEO's high-voltage pep rally.
8. *Make it meaningful.* Tell the mail room clerk why those packages are so important to you. All employees want to feel that their work matters—to you, to their peers, to customers, or to the world.

AGE BIAS AND DISCRIMINATION

Almost no one seems to believe that he or she is biased against the aged, and few would dream of discriminating against the elderly, yet both go on all the time. How can this be? Apparently, even some of us who *think* in ways that respect the rights and needs of older people have some deeply buried prejudice and feelings that pop out in un-guarded moments. Our actions and thoughts may not be congruent, and when we are emotionally stressed, these negative beliefs may escape without our awareness. Most of us have certainly caught our-selves being inconsistent in our response to an older person. In teaching on managing older employees, we have uncovered a thousand different ways in which people express the dichotomy between their feelings and thoughts about elderly people even when they are old themselves.

We think that there is a broad need to publicize age bias and discrimination, our frequent personal participation in them (especially the subconscious aspects), and the varied forms that they take in our society. By raising consciousness, we might use focus groups and similar techniques to lessen the negative effects of such bias, as was done with racial and gender biases decades ago. Such activities certainly do not cure everyone's biases, but they have reduced discrimination and could help many to deal better with their own feelings and thoughts about the aged or about being aged.

We are not suggesting slavish adherence to rules, laws, or guidelines; rather, we encourage exhibiting a positive attitude and creating enthusiasm for making the most of the opportunities offered by older workers.

ORGANIZATIONAL CULTURES AS FUN PARTS OF OUR LIVES

When they were young, many people strove to get a "good" job that offered income, security, prestige, and perhaps a chance for advancement. Often, they never asked, Will I enjoy the work? or Will what I'm doing strengthen my personal sense of worth? or Will it help others? Later, when boredom and a sense of purposelessness set in or when the opportunities faded, some felt almost guilty asking, Is this all there is to working?

The alternative to job dissatisfaction is not an endless round of fun, though the best jobs usually offer some of it. The best jobs may offer satisfying social relationships, recognition, opportunities to achieve, and other satisfactions for a person's spirit. It often seems that most people assess a job on the basis of its external manifestations rather than considering whether they really want to do that work in the long run.

Fortunately, some people do focus on, and find, work that they enjoy and are able to shift to new, more pleasurable jobs if their enthusiasm for certain tasks wears thin. Some people want to use their pension in order to find more pleasurable work or to perform it under more satisfying conditions. Though most of us want "good work," many do not know how to find it, feel that their ability to perform it is limited, and may not even know that it exists for them. Below are some ideas concerning work that could be helpful in managing a society increasingly composed of older workers.

1. We need to see work (the time, energy, and other resources expended to achieve some good) as a natural, integral part of our lives—so natural that though people might want to vary their diet of work, they would no more end it than they would stop eating.
2. What we work at, where we work, how we work, and when we work should (within reason) be more of our own choosing.
3. More people, especially older employees, need to become better educated about themselves—their personalities, their feelings, their special talents, their occupational interests, their attitudes toward work and people, and their general abilities.
4. We may need more of a clear-cut split between how we earn our living and the work we choose to do. Einstein worked in the Swiss patent office at what he called "a shoemaker's job" that paid the bills while he developed his theory of relativity. While we want to gain congruence between ourselves and our work, this may be a longer-term project.

As we settle down for working in the long run, new kinds of workplaces and different organizational cultures could be closer to our concepts of work. In our previous book, *New Corporate Cultures to Motivate*, we called them the "community of leaders" model of culture. These organizations are characterized by a more democratic, inclusive, and mature mode of operation. People share a common culture largely devoid of rank and privilege. We find there substantial openness; willingness to share feelings, ideas, and information; and actual joy (that is, fun) in doing so. People are being trusted and valued; they are seen as generally dependable and responsible; and they are self-managed, confident, and able. Trust means seeing others as legitimate and their needs as valid, which is particularly important for the older person.

But the real fun comes when success and achievements are happening. There is no boss taking the praise when things go well. Being fully in charge gives people a true sense of fulfillment and a great feeling of accomplishment when their decisions have a positive outcome and lead to the next challenge.

ADDRESSING THE NEW REALITIES

As workers and the workplace change, those who treat older workers lightly or brush them aside today are damaging our nation's future. The realities of our changing workforce and its demographics, educational level, and attitudinal characteristics are not to be considered abstract and unimportant and ignored. Employers will have no choice but to address the new realities.

Those who have effectively conserved their aged human resources will be far better equipped to meet tomorrow's challenges than those who have not. The choice is clear. If employers, management, and workers themselves do not solve the problems of older employees, all of us will suffer—not only through social and economic losses that we may never measure adequately but through the decrease in opportunities that we permit.

We have discussed many ways in which employers can encourage older individuals to work longer and stay productive. However, a great deal of imagination will be needed if we are to gain the great potential offered by older employees working late in life. Many (if not most) older employees seek retirement because they are bored or otherwise dissatisfied with their work. Creating a work environment that stimulates interest in continuing may require a fresh look at careers and occupations for older employees. While more of the same old thing may not cut it, fresh ideas may do the trick.

APPENDIX: LEGAL ASPECTS OF WORKING WITH OLDER EMPLOYEES

In recent decades, we have come to see a kind of warfare between some employees and their employers that has been largely waged in the courts. These disputes may affect other people in the workplace and may, in some cases, threaten the future of the organization itself. Legal battles over age discrimination are mostly unnecessary and often self-defeating. Effective and fair management practices could eliminate most suits. The remainder, those initiated for some unrelated ulterior motive of the plaintiff, would be few and largely unsupportable. Yet because of misunderstandings and a tendency to handle adversarial situations in less than competent ways, age-discrimination battles are all too common.

Managers at all levels may flounder when dealing with age issues because mostly they lack clear information on the laws related to age discrimination and how these laws are applied in the workplace. Here we provide a description of the laws, a quick reference guide to their essential aspects, information on how they are being applied, a perspective on the impact of key legal cases on employers, and guidelines for avoiding a charge of age discrimination.

Much of the sharp increase in the number of age-discrimination complaints and lawsuits can be traced to age-based stereotypes and innuendos—mostly by supervisors and managers—as well as ignorance of the law in many organizations. Those problems are often attributable to misunderstandings of the nature of the relationship between age and work performance as well as the legal rights guaranteed older workers by federal and state laws. Thus, a better understanding of the age-related psychological and legal literatures is necessary before the problems their ignorance creates can be overcome. The Age Discrimination in Employment Act (ADEA) aims to achieve age-neutral decisions by management and their organizations, that is, to ensure that hiring, promotion, training, education, and other personnel actions are not influenced by a person's age unless there is a "bona fide occupational qualification" (BFOQ) that overrides the age-neutral intent of the law.

The stated purpose of the ADEA as set out by Congress is

1. to promote employment of older persons based on their ability rather than age;
2. to prohibit arbitrary age discrimination in employment; and
3. to help employers and workers find ways of meeting problems arising from the impact of age on employment.

The act was amended several times, specifically to remove any mandatory age for retirement on most jobs and to prohibit employers from denying benefits to older employees. Thus, the third stated purpose of the statute cited above takes on even greater significance.

There are two ways in which a plaintiff can establish the fact of discrimination. To prove *disparate treatment*, until recently the plaintiff had to show that the discrimination was intentional, but that requirement was removed by a decision of the U.S. Supreme Court on March 30, 2005. Disparate treatment means that the employer purposefully applied terms or conditions of employment that led to less favorable employment consequences for older workers. To prove *disparate impact*, the plaintiff must show that the employment practice(s) in question had a differential effect on older workers regardless of employer intentions.

A brief summary of federal laws and regulations is a good starting point for the discussion of older employees' rights, whether one is an affected worker, a corporate policy setter, a first-line supervisor carrying out those policies, or an executive striving to chart a trouble-free future for his or her organization. A summary of the provisions of the ADEA is presented in Exhibit App.1.

Exceptions and Their Defense

The exceptions to the act as noted in Exhibit App.1—"bona fide occupational qualification" (BFOQ), "reasonable factors other than age," "good

EXHIBIT APP. 1. **Key Provisions of the Age Discrimination in Employment Act (ADEA)**

1. Prohibitions

The act was designed to apply to three entities: (1) employers, (2) employment agencies, and (3) labor organizations. For purposes of the act, employer is defined as any person or business engaged in industry that has "twenty or more employees for each working day in each of twenty or more calendar weeks in the current or preceding calendar year" (29 U.S.C. 630[b]).

Employers are prohibited from (1) refusing to hire or discharging any individual on the basis of his or her age, (2) depriving any employee of employment opportunities because of his or her age, and (3) reducing an older worker's wage rate (29 U.S.C. 623[a]). However, section 631(b)(I) of the act allows employers to mandate retirement of the executive who "for the 2-year period immediately before retirement, is entitled to an annual retirement benefit . . . which equals, in the aggregate, at least $44,000." Tenured college professors and public safety officers are similarly exempted.

Employment agencies are prohibited from either failing to refer for employment or referring for employment any individual because of his or her age (29 U.S.C. 623[b]).

Finally, labor organizations cannot, on the basis of age, (1) expel or exclude any person from their membership, (2) refuse to refer a person for employment or in any other way deprive an individual of employment opportunities, or (3) cause an employer to discriminate against an employee (29 U.S.C. 623[c]).

It is unlawful for any advertisement published by an employer, employment agency, or labor organization to indicate any age preference (29 U.S.C. 623[e]).

2. Exceptions

The act contains three exceptions to the preceding prohibitions. Differentiation based on age is allowed where (1) age is a "bona fide occupational qualification (BFOQ) reasonably necessary to the normal operation of the particular business, or where differentiation is based on reasonable factors other than age," (2) a discharge or disciplinary action is taken for "good cause" (29 U.S.C. 623[f]), or (3) the terms of a bona fide seniority system or any bona fide employee benefit plan, such as a retirement, pension, or insurance plan, are being observed, and these terms are not a "subterfuge to evade the purposes" of the act.

EXHIBIT APP.1 (CONTINUED)

3. Legal Action

The act creates a private right of suit, so that any person aggrieved may bring a civil action, provided that the EEOC does not first decide to file suit on behalf of the individual. The 1978 amendments added to this private right of action the right of the individual to a jury trial (29 U.S.C. 626 [c]).

4. Deadlines for Filing a Lawsuit

No suit can be commenced until the plaintiff has given the EEOC not less than 60 days' notice of intent to file such an action. Such notice shall be filed (1) within 180 days after the alleged unlawful practice occurred or (2) in the event that legal proceedings are initiated under state law, within 300 days after the alleged unlawful practice occurred or within 30 days after receipt by the individual of notice of termination of proceedings under state law, whichever is earlier (29 U.S.C. 626[d]).

5. Statute of Limitations

The running of the time during which an action must be filed is stopped during the period when the EEOC is invoking its right to attempt "voluntary compliance with requirements of this chapter through informal methods of conciliation, conference, and persuasion . . . but in no event for a period in excess of one year" (29 U.S.C. 626[e][2]).

6. Posting of Age-Discrimination Notices

The act requires that every employer, employment agency, and labor organization post, in conspicuous places, notices expressing the purpose of the act (29 U.S.C. 627).

7. Civil Penalties

The court, according to its discretion, can award the plaintiff unpaid minimum wages or unpaid overtime compensation (29 U.S.C. 626[b]), or, in the event that the defendant's violations of the act are deemed willful, the court can order the payment of liquidated damages. Liquidated damages are an amount equal to the plaintiff's award for back pay and fringe benefits; that is, a finding of willfulness results in doubling of the damages. In addition, the court can order "judgments compelling employment, reinstatement or promotion."

EXHIBIT APP.1 (CONTINUED)

8. Criminal Penalties

The act authorizes the imposition of a fine and, where there has been a prior conviction under this statute, imprisonment for not more than one year where an individual impedes the enforcement of the act (29 U.S.C. 629).

---

cause," and the terms of a seniority system or benefit plan that is shown not to be a "subterfuge to evade the purposes" of the act—require further discussion.

When using the first defense, BFOQ in an age-discrimination lawsuit, the employer must be able to make a specific factual showing that employees over age 40 are no longer capable of performing the job in a manner that is "reasonably necessary to the normal operation of the particular business." The employer should not expect a court to simply accept, without proof, that a certain level of good health or physical strength is necessary to satisfactory performance of the job. Obviously, the employer has a much stronger case if it can demonstrate that the BFOQ is needed to protect the public. However, even in cases involving bus drivers and police personnel, the argument of public safety has not always overcome an unconvincing case. Economic considerations also cannot be used to justify decisions based on age where age is not a BFOQ. The employer cannot exclude older workers from a position simply because doing so would be more cost-effective. However, when an employer is forced to reduce the workforce for—generally economic— reasons beyond its control, the discharge of older employees will be considered to be due to "reasonable factors other than age" if the reduction is not primarily of such workers.

The "good cause" exception allows the employer to discharge or discipline an employee, despite being part of a protected class, if it can be shown that age was not a determining factor in the decision. When using the "good cause" exception as a defense in an age-discrimination lawsuit, the employer should be able to present evidence to demonstrate that the employee's performance has fallen below organizational standards that are themselves reasonable and clearly articulated.

It is also important that the employer establish that it followed the customary procedures, known to all employees, when taking disciplinary actions. The key here is consistency and fairness. If the jury finds that the employer's personnel decisions are arbitrarily and inconsistently applied, the case will be lost.

If the exception based on the terms of a seniority system or benefit plan is used as a defense, it requires an examination by the court of whether the system or the plan is "bona fide" and not simply a means of evading the purposes of the act. At least one court has ruled that, with respect to pension plans, the plan that is considered "bona fide"—that is, it is "genuine" and pays adequate benefits—may still be held to be a subterfuge.[1] Generally speaking, in order for a seniority system or benefit plan to be considered a subterfuge, it must treat its older workers in a manner that disadvantages them.

Legal Implications and Lawsuits

Efforts to extend protection to older people or to ensure that they have a fair opportunity to participate in the workforce are not likely to cease in the near future. Many management authorities expect that refinements in the laws related to age discrimination will continue to be made. For example, certain provisions requiring older people to take a physical examination in order to remain employed while younger personnel are not so required have since been outlawed; even people in their 30s can have heart attacks, and if the safety of other people is affected by an employee's physical condition, all such employees should be examined.

Similarly and at the suggestion of the AARP, the Equal Employment Opportunity Commission (EEOC) has rescinded an earlier regulation that prevented older workers from being eligible for apprenticeship programs. This rule was upheld in court, where it was found that while apprenticeship programs were not specifically covered, the ADEA supported application of the law to a variety of workplace relationships.[2] The AARP and other groups are likely to press for other changes in the law as time goes on.

The number of age-discrimination suits has gradually increased over the years, reaching and stabilizing at a level of about 15,000 to 17,000 age-bias complaints per year with the EEOC in the mid-1990s. As an example, the EEOC resolved 15,792 age-discrimination charges in 2004 and recovered $60 million in monetary benefits. Since the basic law allows jury trials, some of the awards given to employees who prove their cases have been very substantial. This can place a great financial burden on organizations that lose.

As a telling example of what may happen, there is the case of Fred Kuehnl, a 56-year-old foreman of a Baltimore, Maryland–based wholesaler of burial caskets who was fired due to age discrimination after 29 years of service. With the EEOC lawsuit dismissed on a grant of summary judgment in the lower court, the EEOC successfully appealed to the U.S. Court of Appeals for the Fourth Circuit, which overturned the dismissal. In the end, the jury decided for Mr. Kuehnl, "a dedicated and loyal employee who worked diligently for 29 years . . . without a single write-up of poor performance." The firing was considered "willful and in reckless disregard of federal law prohibiting age discrimination in employment." The federal jury awarded Mr. Kuehnl $398,000 in back pay and damages, with the EEOC requesting an injunction to prohibit the company from future acts of age discrimination.

In another jury trial, Richard Miller, who had sued his former employer, a real estate group, alleging unlawful age discrimination and retaliation, was awarded by the jury $232,000 for willful discrimination and breach of contract, while the court added another $330,000 for front pay, attorney's fees, and costs—an expensive breach of the law, which was subsequently affirmed by the appeals court, holding that Richard Miller "provided sufficient evidence upon which the jury could reasonably conclude that the realtor's stated reasons for termination were pretexts for discrimination."

Who Sues?

Today, there is sufficient public awareness of the law and of the most important elements of age discrimination so that employees will generally take action and file a complaint if so aggrieved. As a matter of fact, most public and many private organizations have established procedures, venues, or Web sites to make the process easy to manage. It seems important to focus attention on early warning signs of such discrimination in order to avoid the surprise of major litigation.

If it comes to a lawsuit, many factors influence who takes the case to court. Lawsuits tend to be expensive, and it has been claimed that the cost of court cases weeds out all victims except the middle-class manager who's financially capable of filing a lawsuit. However, with the act providing for doubling of back pay and liquidated damages, more lawyers are willing to take the more solid cases on the basis of speculation. Even so, the cases of older managers and professionals are most appealing, because older workers with more seniority are usually better paid, so that back pay awards to them would be correspondingly higher. Mark deBernardo, a labor lawyer for the U.S. Chamber of Commerce, has been quoted as saying that the prospect of double damages has created "a lotto mentality" among older workers and some lawyers who seek "astronomical awards." He cited a $2.4 million judgment against the I. Magnin clothing stores for dismissing three older workers in California.

The rise in discrimination complaints has also been attributed to the growing number of workers covered by the law. In recent years, the major force behind the increasing challenges to age discrimination has been our national economy undergoing structural changes and the growing number of older workers protected by ADEA. The shift from an industrial to a service economy—accompanied by mergers, buyouts and restructuring, and production jobs migrating to foreign countries—has put many older employees out of work, prematurely and unfairly, in the view of many observers. These structural changes have affected an unprecedented proportion of managerial and professional people, the very people most able and likely to file an ADEA suit.

Litigation is not limited to older employees, however, in the sense of the general understanding of that term. In a recent court case of about 200 employees against General Dynamics Land Systems, Inc. the plaintiffs—each of them between the ages of 40 and 49 on July 1, 1997—alleged that a provision of health benefits, which was part of a new bargaining agreement that was to benefit only workers over the age of 50 on July 1, 1997, constituted illegal discrimination based on age. While the district court dismissed the suit with the surprising conclusion that ADEA did not recognize claims for "reverse discrimination," the appeals court reversed the decision, holding that the claimants were, in effect, members of the ADEA's protected class and that the language of the statute had an "unambiguous and clear meaning," not permitting the courts to redraft it. "Therefore, the protected class should be protected; to hold otherwise [would be] discrimination, plain and simple."

Who Wins?

The most important aspect of who wins or loses is the issue of credible testimony and the quality of the "proof" on each side. Organizations tend to lose suits because they can't establish that an employee's work justified dismissal. But even with good personnel records, cases often boil down to credibility contests.

In a well-documented classic case involving *Miles, Inc.* the jury awarded $1.63 million to nine older workers dismissed in a company-wide layoff. Miles had inherited the age-bias charges when it merged with Cutter Laboratories and claimed that $60 million in losses had forced Cutter to lay off 1,200 employees and that it picked the least productive people with the worst sales records. The plaintiffs claimed that the company's performance standards were biased against people over 40. The clincher in the workers' case was that they were able to produce records showing that they had received glowing performance evaluations in recent years. So who wins or loses is often a matter of who is most believable.

In another case of a female employee against *Northrop Grumman*, both the judge in the case and the appeals court ruled in favor of the employer. The employee had lost her job in a "reduction in force" (RIF), which she did not question in terms of its "bona fide" aspects. She claimed, however, that a younger fellow worker was given discriminatory preference over her by being "bumped" into another job, while she did not have that opportunity. However, the handbook distributed to all of the company's employees clearly stated that bumping rights required an application for the job one wanted to be bumped into, and the fellow worker had in fact applied for the new job. Therefore, her claim of discrimination was found to have no merit.

While some areas of the law are still being mapped, a vast number of cases have moved through the courts to give lawyers and personnel specialists a good idea of what constitutes age discrimination and what does and doesn't work in pursuing or fighting such charges. This would indicate that fewer questionable cases would actually reach the courts, but that does not necessarily mean fewer cases. By the end of the decade, more than half the workforce will be people age 40 and over who will be protected by the law.

Lawyers claim that the current interest in age-discrimination suits may be nothing compared to what lies ahead. They expect that more older people with medical handicaps are likely to file suits under handicap as well as age provisions of the law. In addition, more older blacks and women will be contending for jobs held by older white men. Age-bias suits are predicted to be among the five hottest liabilities facing business in the next ten years. New questions are likely to arise as the workforce and supporting organizations become more sophisticated. For instance, one might imagine that voluntary early retirement plans may be seen as subtly coercive and that the fast-track method of management, in which younger "bright stars" are transferred from department to department to broaden their experience, may be considered illegal.

As an example of that kind of different view of age discrimination, we would like to mention here a recent lawsuit filed by the EEOC against the Chicago law firm of Sidley Austin Brown & Wood. In the past, certain partners of the law firm had, at certain times, been involuntarily downgraded and expelled from the partnership on account of their age and also in part pursuant to a mandatory retirement policy. The EEOC had determined that "except for a few controlling partners at the very top, [the firm's] lawyers appeared to be ordinary employees not unlike their colleagues at parallel levels in the business community and, therefore, covered by the ADEA." Therefore, the law firm was seen in violation of the act and taken to court.

A Cooperative Approach

The job of management and workers is to produce, not to fight. Hundreds of major American organizations have never been the target of an ADEA complaint, let alone involved in such a lawsuit. This is because they train their supervisors well in resolving conflicts in a truly win-win fashion. Obviously, they also train their supervisors not to discriminate, but if they are challenged in a specific case, they have a host of sophisticated, nonmanipulative ways to work out their differences so that the relationship strengthens rather than deteriorates.

By contrast, many employees, managers, and their organizations are stuck with a focus on confrontational, adversarial approaches to getting their own way or proving that they are right, rather than on cooperative ways of respecting others and dealing effectively with conflict. Managers who provoke or engage in combat, rather than using their energies, resources, and time to produce, lessen the efficiency and general competitiveness of their organizations. Employees who slack off or are passive when they experience discrimination and then "go for the gold" when they do confront the organization with a lawsuit are playing the same game.

Though there are always two sides to any conflict, the organization has the primary responsibility for ensuring age-neutral employment actions. When employees are treated unfairly, the quality of life for them and everyone around them is degraded. If that happens often, the quality of life in our society is equally degraded. A company can no longer discriminate on the basis of age (or any other legally prohibited factor) without having to expect consequences. The other employees are watching and will respond negatively—you can count on that. Reprisals against employees no longer keep the others in line as they might have at one time. While that tactic might have worked earlier in the past century, when management efforts were often directed toward turning employees into machine components, in this emerging age of knowledge workers, where productivity is in the mind of the employee, such action is self-defeating and outdated.

The proliferation of ADEA cases is not likely to subside in the near future as our workforce continues aging. At the same time, we must consider that the loss of an ADEA case can damage an organization's public image. In addition, ADEA has an obvious impact even on the organization's younger workers. If it is not clear that the organization's practices are fair, not only may companies find that their younger workers seek their fortunes elsewhere, but affirmative action developmental programs for women and minorities may be stalled. Developing optimum policies for all employees should be a priority and may in some instances take considerable imagination.

Without the age cap of 70, workers are likely to become accustomed to the notion that *any* age-based personnel action affecting a person over age 40 is subject to serious challenge. Effective, age-neutral management behaviors and policies are likely to be increasingly important to organizational success.

NOTES

CHAPTER 1

1. Peter F. Drucker, "The Coming of the New Organization," *Harvard Business Review* (Jan.–Feb. 1988): 45–53.

2. Adolf Haasen and Gordon F. Shea, *New Corporate Cultures That Motivate* (Westport: Praeger, 2003).

3. R. Stephens, "New Hurdles at Work: Technology, Rising Health Costs Hurt Older Workers," *AARP Bulletin* 30, no. 11 (1990): 1, 4–5.

CHAPTER 2

1. Mitra Toossi, "A Century of Change: The U.S. Labor Force, 1950–2050," *Monthly Labor Review* (May 2002): 15–28.

2. Mitra Toossi, "Labor Force Projections to 2012: The Graying of the U.S. Workforce," *Monthly Labor Review* (Feb. 2004): 37–57.

3. Michael Horrigan, "Employment Projections to 2012: Concepts and Context," *Monthly Labor Review* (Feb. 2004): 3–22.

4. "How Sick Is Social Security?" *Wall Street Journal*, June 28, 2004, R1–4.

5. "Ageing Societies and the Looming Pension Crisis," *OECD* (May 2004): 1–3.

CHAPTER 3

1. Howard Gardner, *Creating Minds: An Anatomy of Creativity Seen through the Lives of Freud, Einstein, Picasso, Stravinsky, Eliot, Graham and Gandhi* (Reprint, New York: Basic Books, 1994).

CHAPTER 4

1. B. Rosen, "Management Perceptions of Older Employees," *Monthly Labor Review* 10, no. 5 (1978): 33–35.

2. R. L. Coser, "Old Age, Employment and Social Networks," In *The Aging Employee*, ed. Stanley F. Yolles et al. (New York: Human Sciences Press, 1984), pp. 131–132.

3. David A. Peterson, *Facilitating Education for Older Learners* (San Francisco: Jossey-Bass, 1983).

4. Harry S. Maas and Jose A. Kuypers, *From Thirty to Seventy: A Forty-Year Longitudinal Study of Adult Lifestyles and Personality* (San Francisco: Jossey-Bass, 1974).

5. Stephanie FallCreek and Molly Mettler, *A Healthy Old Age: A Sourcebook for Health Promotion with Older Adults* (New York: Haworth Press, 1984).

6. L. G. Rayburn, "Relationship between Corporate Financial Performance and Executive Age," *Mid-South Business Journal* 3, no. 1 (1983): 12–16.

7. Ken Dychtwald and Joe Flower, *Age Wave: The Challenges and Opportunities of an Aging America* (New York: Bantam Books, 1990): 92–99.

CHAPTER 5

1. YourEncore, Inc. at www.yourencore.com.

2. Norman Root, "Injuries at Work Are Fewer among Older Workers," *Monthly Labor Review* 104, no. 3 (1981): 30–34.

3. J. Fields, "Does Life Exist for Copywriters over 45? You Are Only as Old as You Think You Are," *Advertising Age* (1978).

4. Marc Freedman, "Take Advantage of Us." *civicventures.org* (Fall 2004).

5. Ron Zemke, Claire Raines, and Bob Filipczak, *Generations at Work: Managing the Clash of Veterans, Boomers, Xers and Nexters in Your Workplace* (New York: AMACOM, 1999).

CHAPTER 6

1. L. D. Haber, "Age and Capacity Devaluation," *Journal of Health and Social Behavior* 11, no. 3 (1970): 167–182.

2. P. L. Rones, "Older Men: The Choice between Work and Retirement," *Monthly Labor Review* 101, no. 11 (1978): 3–10.

3. J. P. McCann, "Control Data's 'Stay Well' Program," *Training and Development Journal* (Oct. 1981): 39–43.

4. W. R. Miller, "Pharmaceuticals for the Elderly," *Vital Speeches* 52, no. 13 (1986): 396–398.

CHAPTER 7

1. National Older Worker Career Center, "Myths and Reality" (Survey of the Committee of Economic Development), reported at www.nowcc.org (2004).

2. Ibid. (the Media Audit).

3. Harvey L. Sterns, "Integrating Work and Learning: A Key to Older Employee Success," *Business & Aging Networker* (Winter 2001): 1.

4. Ibid., 2.

5. Ibid.

6. Ibid., 1–2.

7. Ibid., 2.

8. Ibid.

9. Ibid.

CHAPTER 9

1. L. E. Dube, "Removing the Cap: Eliminating Mandatory Retirement under the ADEA," *Employment Relations Today* (Autumn 1988): 203–204.

2. *Gill v. Union Carbide* (E.D. Tenn. 1973).

CHAPTER 10

1. See also Brad Humphrey, "The 21st Century Supervisor," *HR Magazine* (May 2000): 83–85.

CHAPTER 11

1. William G. Dyer, *Team Building: Issues and Alternatives* (Reading: Addison-Wesley, 1987).

2. G. Codrington, "Training the Generations," *TomorrowToday.biz* (2003).

3. S. Sekiguchi, "How Japanese Business Treats Its Older Workers," *Management Review* (Oct. 1980): 15–18.

4. Victoria Kaminski, "New Personnel Specialty," *Personnel Administrator* (Aug. 1983).

CHAPTER 12

1. Susan A. Mohrman, *A Perspective on Empowerment* (Los Angeles: CEO Publications/University of Southern California, May 1993).

2. Billy Arcement, "Job Satisfaction Starts with an Enthusiastic Attitude," *Greater Baton Rouge Business Report* (Apr. 24, 2001).

3. Douglas McGregor, *The Human Side of Enterprise* (New York: McGraw-Hill, 1960).

CHAPTER 13

1. Sarah Fister Gale, "Phased Retirement," *Workforce Management* (2004), www.workforce.com.

2. Ibid.

3. Helen Ginsburg, "Flexible and Partial Retirement for Norwegian and Swedish Workers," *Monthly Labor Review* 108, no. 10 (1985): 33–34.

4. Ken Dychtwald and Joe Flower, *Age Wave: The Challenges and Opportunities of an Aging America* (New York: Bantam Books, 1990).

CONCLUSION

1. Federal Reserve Bank of Cleveland, "Education and the Workforce," *Economic Trends* (Oct. 2004).

2. Kathy Gurchiek, "Survey: Exodus Follows an Improving Economy," *HR Magazine* (Mar. 2005).

3. Jyoti Thottam, "Thank God It's Monday," *Time* (Jan. 17, 2005): 58–61.

APPENDIX

1. *EEOC* v. *Home Insurance Co.* (D.C.N.Y., 1982).

2. *EEOC* v. *Seafarers Intl Union* (4th Cir. 394 F. 3d. 197).

SELECTED BIBLIOGRAPHY

Arcement, Billy. "Job Satisfaction Starts with an Enthusiastic Attitude." *Greater Baton Rouge Business Report* (Apr. 24, 2001).

Bakaly, C. G., and J. M. Grossman. "How to Avoid Wrongful Discharge Suits." *Management Review* (Aug. 1984): 41–46.

Bakke, Dennis W. *Joy at Work: A Revolutionary Approach to Fun on the Job.* Seattle: PVG, 2005.

Bolles, Richard Nelson. "The Decade of Decisions." *Modern Maturity* (Feb./Mar. 1990): 36–46.

———. *What Color Is Your Parachute?* Berkeley: Ten Speed, 1988.

Codrington, G. "Training the Generations." *TomorrowToday.biz* (2003).

Cohen, Gene D. *The Creative Age.* New York: Harper Paperbacks, 2001.

Colburn, D. "Retirement Redefined." *Washington Post*, Mar. 6, 1985: 12–14.

Cook, D. D. "Older Workers: A Resource We'll Need." *Industry Week* (1980): 42–48.

Coser, R. L. "Old Age, Employment and Social Networks." In *The Aging Employee*, ed. Stanley F. Yolles et al. New York: Human Sciences Press, 1984, pp. 131–132.

Crichtley, Robert K. *Rewired, Rehired or Retired?* San Francisco: Pfeiffer, 2002.

Csikszentmihaly, Mihaly. *Flow: The Psychology of Optimal Experience.* New York: Harper & Row, 1990.

Drucker, Peter F. "The Coming of the New Organization." *Harvard Business Review* (Jan./Feb. 1988): 45–53.

Dube, L. E. "Removing the Cap: Eliminating Mandatory Retirement under the ADEA." *Employment Relations Today* (Autumn 1988): 199–264.

Dychtwald, Ken. *Age Power: How the 21st Century Will Be Ruled by the New Old.* New York: Tarcher/Putnam, 1999.

Dychtwald, Ken, and Joe Flower. *Age Wave: The Challenges and Opportunities of an Aging America.* New York: Bantam Books, 1990.

Dyer, William G. *Team Building: Issues and Alternatives.* Reading: Addison-Wesley, 1987.

FallCreek, Stephanie, and Molly Mettler. *A Healthy Old Age: A Sourcebook for Health Promotion with Older Adults.* New York: Haworth Press, 1984.

Fister Gale, Sarah. "Phased Retirement." *Workforce Management* (2004). www.workforce.com.

Freedman, Marc. *Prime Time: How Baby Boomers Will Revolutionize Retirement and Transform America.* Reprint. New York: Public Affairs, 2002.

Gardner, Howard. *Creating Minds: An Anatomy of Creativity Seen through the Lives of Freud, Einstein, Picasso, Stravinsky, Eliot, Graham and Gandhi.* Reprint. New York: Basic Books, 1994.

Ginsburg, Helen. "Flexible and Partial Retirement for Norwegian and Swedish Workers." *Monthly Labor Review* 108, no. 10 (1985): 33–34.

Goldberg, Beverly. *Age Works: What America Must Do to Survive the Graying of the Workforce.* New York: Free Press, 2002.

Gurchiek, Kathy. "Survey: Exodus Follows an Improving Economy." *HR Magazine* (Mar. 2005).

Haasen, Adolf, and Gordon F. Shea. *A Better Place to Work.* New York: American Management Association, 1997.

———. *New Corporate Cultures That Motivate.* Westport: Praeger, 2003.

Haber, L. D. "Age and Capacity Devaluation." *Journal of Health and Social Behavior* 11, no. 3 (1970): 167–182.

Hackman, J. Richard. *Groups That Work (and Those That Don't).* San Francisco: Jossey-Bass, 1990.

Herzberg, Frederick. "One More Time: How Do You Motivate Employees?" *Harvard Business Review* (Sept./Oct. 1987): 109–120.

Herzberg, Frederick, Bernard Mausner, and Barbara Beoch Snyderman. *The Motivation to Work.* New York: Wiley, 1959.

Horrigan, Michael. "Employment Projections to 2012: Concepts and Context." *Monthly Labor Review* (Feb. 2004): 3–22.

Humphrey, Brad. "The 21st Century Supervisor." *HR Magazine* (May 2000): 83–85.

Kaminski, Victoria. "New Personnel Specialty." *Personnel Administrator* (Aug. 1983): 36–39.

Knowles, Malcolm. *The Adult Learner: A Neglected Species.* Houston: Gulf Publishing, 1981.

Kotlikoff, Laurence J., and Scott Burns. *The Coming Generational Storm: What You Need to Know about America's Economic Future.* Cambridge: MIT Press, 2004.

Lucas, James R. *The Passionate Organization.* New York: American Management Association, 1999.

Maas, Harry S., and Joseph A. Kuypers. *From Thirty to Seventy: A Forty-Year Longitudinal Study of Adult Lifestyles and Personality.* San Francisco: Jossey-Bass, 1974.

Macleod, J. S. "Facing the Issue of Age Discrimination." *Employment Relations Today* (Fall 1983): 57–62.

Maslow, Abraham H. *Motivation and Personality.* New York: Harper & Row, 1954.

McCann, J. P. "Control Data's 'Stay Well' Program." *Training and Development Journal* (Oct. 1981).

McClelland, David C., and David G. Winter. *Motivating Economic Achievement.* New York: Free Press, 1969.

McGregor, Douglas. *The Human Side of Enterprise.* New York: McGraw-Hill, 1960.

Mohrman, Susan A. *A Perspective on Empowerment.* CEO Publications/USC, May 1993.

Peterson, David A. *Facilitating Education for Older Learners.* San Francisco: Jossey-Bass, 1983.

Rayburn, L. G. "Relationship between Corporate Financial Performance and Executive Age." *Mid-South Business Journal* 3, no. 1 (1983): 12–16.

Rones, P. L. "Older Men: The Choice between Work and Retirement." *Monthly Labor Review* 101, no. 11 (Nov. 1978): 3–10.

Rosen, B. "Management Perceptions of Older Employees." *Monthly Labor Review* 10, no. 5 (1978): 33–35.

Sadler, William A. *The Third Age.* Reprint. Cambridge: Perseus, 2001.

Schuster, M. H., and C. S. Miller. "Performance Evaluations as Evidence in ADEA Cases." *Employee Relations Law Journal* (June 1981): 561–583.

Sekiguchi, S. "How Japanese Business Treats Its Older Workers." *Management Review* (Oct. 1980): 15–18.

Sheppard, H. L. "The Relevance of Age to Worker Behavior in the Labor Market." *Industrial Gerontology* (Summer 1972): 1–11.

Stephens, R. "New Hurdles at Work: Technology, Rising Health Costs Hurt Older Workers." *AARP Bulletin* 30, no. 11 (1990): 1, 4–5.

Sterns, Harvey L. "Integrating Work and Learning: A Key to Older Employee Success." *Business & Aging Networker* (Winter 2001).

Thottam, Jyoti. "Thank God It's Monday." *Time* (Jan. 17, 2005): 58–61.

Toossi, Mitra. "A Century of Change: The U.S. Labor Force 1950–2050." *Monthly Labor Review* (May 2002): 15–28.

———. "Labor Force Projections to 2012: The Graying of the U.S. Workforce." *Monthly Labor Review* (Feb. 2004): 37–57.

Walker, Jean Erickson. *The Age Advantage: Making the Most of Your Midlife Career Transition.* New York: Penguin, 2000.

Wallace, Paul. *Agequake: Riding the Demographic Rollercoaster Shaking Business, Finance and Our World.* London: Brealey, 1999.

Webber, R. A. "Homogeneous Groups." *Academy of Management Journal* 17 (1974): 570–573.

Zemke, Ron, Claire Raines, and Bob Filipczak. *Generations at Work: Managing the Clash of Veterans, Boomers, Xers and Nexters in Your Workplace.* New York: AMACOM, 1999.

INDEX

ABOUT THE AUTHORS

GORDON F. SHEA is founder of Prime Systems Company, a training and human resources firm in the Washington/Baltimore area. He holds a BA from Syracuse University and an MA from George Washington University. Shea has been a practicing supervisor, manager, and executive for over 30 years in government and private industry.

Shea has authored 16 books and over 700 articles on such topics as leadership and management, hiring and retention of new employees, mentoring, workplace development, creative negotiating, trust, loyalty, and ethics.

In recent years, Shea has focused on initiatives that help to strengthen both the workplace and the workforce, providing clients with a competitive edge in today's business environment.

Shea also serves as Adjunct Assistant Professor in the Department of Communications at the University of Maryland University College (UMUC). This institution is the premier worldwide educational arm of UM, selected in 1947 by the U.S. Armed Forces Institute to facilitate educational courses wherever U.S. military personnel and their civilian support staff are stationed outside the United States.

ADOLF HAASEN is managing partner of A&R Associates, a human resources consulting firm based in Hartsdale, New York. Before founding A&R Associates, he gained extensive international management experience as an executive for the German Merck organization. Haasen joined Merck in his native Germany and, a few years later, was assigned to Merck subsidiaries in Brazil and in Colombia, South America. Subsequently, he became CEO of EM Industries, Merck's U.S. subsidiary, which he headed for 20 years, taking it from a small start-up to a $200 million company with about 800 employees.

Having lived for many years in several different countries and having extensively traveled in others, Haasen not only is fluent in German, English, Spanish, and Portuguese but has acquired significant knowledge and familiarity with European, Latin American, and U.S. cultures. This has been a unique and fortunate opportunity not only to meet people from diverse backgrounds but to get acquainted with art and literature of varied origins.

While at EM Industries, Haasen took particular interest in the human resources area, developing new management talent and providing a climate of openness and trust that enabled EM to substantially grow its business during his 20-year tenure. His current consulting and research interests focus on workplace motivation and unique workplace environments that foster employee participation and self-management.

Haasen has a degree from the Max Planck Gymnasium in Goettingen, Germany, as well as a business diploma from the Chamber of Industry and Commerce in Darmstadt, Germany. With his longtime friend and business associate Gordon F. Shea, he authored *A Better Place to Work* (1997) and *New Corporate Cultures That Motivate* (Praeger, 2003). In addition, Haasen has written several articles on unique workplace cultures.